FLORENCE HAS WON MY HEART

FLORENCE HAS WON MY HEART

*Literary visitors to
the Tuscan capital,
1750-1950*

Mark Roberts

Anthony Eyre
MOUNT ORLEANS PRESS

Published in Great Britain in 2024
by Anthony Eyre, Mount Orleans Press
23 High Street, Cricklade SN6 6AP
https://anthonyeyre.com

ISBN 978-1-912945-43-6

A CIP record for this book is available
from the British Library

Set in 12/14pt Dante MT

Printed in Malta by
Gutenberg Press

Uxori carissimae liberisque dilectissimis

CONTENTS

PREFACE

THE PHRASE 'Florence has won my heart' was uttered by the banker and poet Samuel Rogers (1763-1855), who decided that 'in Florence I should wish to live, beyond all the cities of the world'. My own heart was won by Florence early in 1971, when I came between school and university in order to look at the art and to study Italian. I put up at the family-run Pensione Antica in via Pandolfini, and enrolled on an Italian course at the British Institute. There were very few tourists in the month of March, and the museums and galleries were empty. Notebook in hand, I embarked on a rigid programme of sightseeing, conscious of being a part of a long line of amateur English sightseers in the Tuscan capital. At one stage the Uffizi and the other state museums were closed because of a strike: *sciopero* was a hideous word that I came to detest. That particular strike did not last long, however, and in any case there are more than 100 churches which in those days opened very early and stayed open until noon. In my sightseeing excursions, punctuated by Italian lessons and by delicious meals at the pensione, I came to know and love—either then or later—the angel candlestick to the right of the altar in the Baptistery; the frescoes of the life of St Sylvester by Maso di Banco, in the Bardi di Vernio Chapel at Santa Croce; Tino di Camaino's statue of *Caritas*, with two babies scrambling at her breasts, in the Museo Bardini; the cool, dark interior of the church of Santi Apostoli, where I would be married; the exceptionally sumptuous and gorgeous Madonna and Child by Andrea Vanni in the Uffizi; Francesco Furini's erotically charged painting of *Hylas and the Nymphs*, in Palazzo Pitti; the diptych ascribed to Simone Martini in the Horne Museum; Fra Angelico's exquisite *Madonna della Stella*, at San Marco; the harmonious façade of Palazzo Bartolini-Salimbeni, in piazza Santa Trìnita; the Cardinal of Portugal's chapel at San Miniato; Verrocchio's Lavabo, and Donatello's bronze pulpits, at San Lorenzo; the ivory of *Adam Naming the Beasts*, in the

Bargello; the dog's footprints on the tiles of Brunelleschi's dome of Santa Maria del Fiore, which resemble the ones on the ceiling of our kitchen; the panel by Giovanni Dolciati, in the Stibbert Museum, narrating in nine episodes the sad story of Antonio Rinaldeschi; the sublime Della Robbia angels that kneel either side of the Blessed Sacrament in Santa Maria del Fiore; the statue of the game of *saccomazzone*, in Boboli; 'Mr and Mrs Etruscan', on their conjugal sarcophagus, in the Museo Archeologico; the portable altar, bearing the symbols of the four Evangelists, in the Museo degli Argenti in Palazzo Pitti; the lozenge-shaped panel illustrating the sacrament of the Eucharist, in the Opera del Duomo museum, and the magnificent embroidered panels to designs by Antonio del Pollaiuolo, in the same museum; the Ponte Santa Trìnita at night, or in the blazing July sunlight; the fresco of the *Birth of the Virgin*, by Andrea del Sarto, in the narthex of the Santissima Annunziata; the Neptune Fountain in piazza della Signoria, so much admired by my late painter friend Richard Serrin; the anonymous portrait of the Aztec emperor Moctezuma, in Palazzo Pitti; the fresco of St Peter healing the cripples with his shadow, in the Brancacci Chapel at the Carmine, by Masaccio; Donatello's so-called *Atys*, in the Bargello; the mosaic, transported from Old St Peter's in Rome to the Florentine church of San Marco, showing the Virgin Mother of God as *Mater Misericordiae*; the airy proportions of the church of San Salvatore al Monte, Michelangelo's *bella villanella*, used as the model for a room in the Berlin Museums; the monument to the hard-working donkey, or mule, in the Pitti courtyard; Titian's *La Bella*, in the Palatine Gallery, and his *Venus of Urbino*, in the Uffizi; and other beautiful sights too numerous to list. Six years after my initial visit (when the city still smelt to some extent of the *nafta* or central-heating fuel carried on the waters of the disastrous 1966 flood), I returned to Florence on the strength of an offer of work at the British Institute. My fiancée and I imagined we would stay perhaps five years, but that was reckoning without the subtle and cumulative attraction that the city exerts on minds such as ours. We married in July 1977 and had five children, all born in Tuscany. It is to them and to their mother that this book is dedicated.

INTRODUCTION

THE FIRST Anglo-Florentine—that is to say the first Englishman we know of to have had an extended connection with the city—was JOHN HAWKWOOD, who was born around 1320 at Sible Headingham in Essex. He came to Italy in 1361 and two years later was elected Captain-General of the White Company, a frightening band of mercenaries who polished their weapons and armour with marrow extracted from the broken legs of goats. He was famous for the astonishing rapidity of his movements, and for his murderous efficiency. From 2 February 1377, for three days and nights, he perpetrated the terrible massacre of Cesena, when some 6,000 ordinary men, women and children were barbarously

Above: John Hawkwood, by Paolo Uccello

9

slaughtered. Hawkwood became commander of the Florentine troops in 1378, and in April 1391 he was made an honorary citizen of Florence. They could not pronounce his name so they called him Giovanni Acuto, or 'Sharp John'. After his death in 1394 his body was given a magnificent torchlit state funeral (it lay on a bier adorned with gold brocades and vermillion velvets) before being sent back to Essex, at the personal request of King Richard II. Paolo Uccello's equestrian portrait of him in the left aisle of Florence Cathedral shows his horse walking with both right legs advanced, something a real horse seldom does.

In later centuries several English visitors came to Florence, some of whom registered their impressions in fascinating detail. They included the humanist John Colet, the poet John Milton, the diarist John Evelyn and the priest and travel writer Richard Lassels, who coined the phrase 'Grand Tour'. (This is the conventional term for the educational voyages around Europe undertaken by the sons of the English, Irish and Scottish nobility and gentry, who were generally accompanied by a travelling tutor.)

By the mid-eighteenth century the trickle of British visitors had become a stream. Northern Europeans, and especially the British, have been coming regularly to Florence for some three centuries. During the period of the so-called Grand Tour, rich and not-so-rich travellers were welcomed at the hospitable table of Sir Horace Mann, the British diplomatic representative at the Grand Ducal court, who resided for over forty years in the Casa Manetti in via Santo Spirito. The poet Thomas Gray called Mann 'the best and most obliging person in the world', and it was because of Mann that Grand Tourists were much less likely to linger in Venice, or to press on to Rome or Naples, than they might otherwise have been. Florence was the thing. Not long after Horace Mann died in 1788, the French Revolutionary Wars put an end to continental travel for the British. When travel resumed after the defeat of Napoleon at Waterloo in 1815, it was a markedly less aristocratic and more bourgeois affair, with tours being later arranged by the enterprising offices of Thomas Cook.

Throughout the nineteenth century there was a pronounced literary and artistic component to the English presence in Tuscany. The second wave of Romantic poets—Byron, Shelley and Keats—all came to live in Italy, and Shelley wrote his celebrated 'Ode to the West Wind' in the Florentine park of the Cascine. What was it that drew these northern visitors? There would seem to have been four main attractions. One was the climate: the 'blue Italian day' made such a pleasing contrast to grey northern drizzle. Florence was 'a sunny place for shady people' (a phrase that has been applied to other places as well, such as Monte Carlo and Costa Rica). The second attraction was indeed the comparative sexual liberty: one has the impression that gay and Lesbian couples formed a higher-than-average proportion of the expatriate community, and homosexuality was not often prosecuted or punished in Italy. Adultery was tolerated. Thirdly, the cost of living in Florence was considerably lower than in London, and in the city's numerous pensions and small hotels it was possible to live for many months at trifling expense. The last and perhaps greatest attraction was the art. For in Florence were to be found the models—most especially, the paintings of Sandro Botticelli—for the Pre-Raphaelite school of painters, who had been encouraged by the critical writings of John Ruskin. Many members of this school visited or settled in Florence—Lord Leighton, G.F. Watts, Edward Burne-Jones, Walter Crane and Charles Fairfax Murray, to name a few. On 17 June 1898, only hours before his death, Burne-Jones told his visitor Frieda Stanhope that 'Florence is everything and all the rest is nothing.' Most eminent among the writers who came here were Walter Savage Landor, Arthur Hugh Clough and Elizabeth Barrett Browning, all three of whom lie buried in the so-called English cemetery in piazzale Donatello, which is actually owned by the Swiss.

In the twentieth century writers continued to flock to Florence. It is most unlikely that the stream has dried up in the twenty-first century, but that is beyond the scope of this book.

I have restricted myself to visitors from the English-speaking world, so I have reluctantly ignored Dostoyevsky, Montaigne, Stendhal, Hesse, Andersen, Mommsen and numerous others. The visitors are arranged in chronological order by date of birth. I have included a few non-literary ones, and a few who were not visitors because born in Florence.

Johan Zoffany The Tribuna of the Uffizi, 1772-77

I

THE LATER EIGHTEENTH CENTURY

WHEN THE LAST Medici Grand Duke, the dissolute and childless Gian Gastone, died in 1737, the European powers ensured that he was succeeded by Franz Stefan, duke of Lorraine, who thus became Francesco II of Tuscany. He and his wife Maria Teresa stayed in the city for only three months, before decamping for good to Vienna, leaving Tuscany in the hands of a Council of Regency, so that all his Florentine subjects got to see of their sovereign was his statue prancing on a horse on top of the triumphal gateway in what is now piazza della Libertà; perhaps not many people know that the great and beautiful Maria Teresa was once Grand Duchess of Tuscany; in 1745 Franz Stefan was elected Holy Roman Emperor and Archduke of Austria, though he remained Grand Duke of Tuscany for the rest of his life.

The diplomat HORACE MANN (1706-1786) was the leading Anglo-Florentine of the eighteenth century, and the cynosure of the Grand Tourists. His first visit to Italy was on account of his health, in the years 1732-1733; so dim was the view he took of his chances of survival that he brought his own coffin with him on the journey; he was always rather a hypochondriac, or at any rate a valetudinarian. Luckily he did survive this initial brush with Italy, and indeed made some useful contacts. Five years later he was back in Italy, in Florence, where in 1738 he became the assistant to Charles Fane, at that time Envoy Extraordinary and Minister Plenipotentiary to the Tuscan court, whose duties he effectively took over. The Honble Charles Fane was a very lazy and rather highly-strung person, and was said to have taken to his bed for six weeks after the Duke of Newcastle, in one of his letters, forgot to sign himself 'Your very humble servant', as usual, and only put 'Your humble servant.' Horace Mann on the other hand was universally admired for his pleasant manners and

British gentlemen at Sir Horace Mann's house in Florence, *by Thomas Patch, ca 1765*

accommodating nature. His kindness was generally acknowledged, perhaps most admiringly by the 5th Earl of Cork and Orrery: 'he does honour to our nation. He lives elegantly and generously. He never fails in any point of civility and kindness to his countrymen. The politeness of his manners, and the prudence of his conduct, are shining examples both to the Britons and Italians. He is the only person I have ever known, whom all Englishmen agree in praising.' On the Italian side, Filippo Mazzei paid tribute to '*l'eccellente carattere del detto Signor Orazio Mann*', and referred to Mann's '*cuore angelico*' and said he was '*incapace di mentire volontariamente*', which is all the more convincing as Mazzei was a supporter of the American colonists and at the time of writing was on the opposite side from Mann in the War of Independence. The amorous adventurer and libertine Giacomo Casanova described Mann as '*l'idole de Florence, homme fort riche, aimable quoique Anglais, plein d'esprit et de goût et grand amateur des arts*' (Mann would be startled to be described as very rich, since he was always complaining about his salary being in arrears and of a general shortage of funds). Mann allowed his English spongers to sit around all morning in his house reading the newspapers, and he entertained most lavishly. His official residence was the Casa Manetti, on the south side of via Santo Spirito, but he had another house, on the same side of the river, known as the Casa Ambrogi, where he quite often put up his visitors. In his letters to Walpole, Mann occasionally complains about his English parasites: the 'hundred who only come to scramble for sherbets and to pocket the glasses.' And he describes his own somewhat odd daily routine: he rose at 7.30, ate 4 or 5 oz of lamb's brains, then some soup and some stewed peaches. He went back to bed at half past two in the afternoon, and 'at about 6.30 I drink tea for the sake of the bread and butter I eat with it… I receive company in the garden and am famous for the best lemonade in Florence.'

HORACE WALPOLE (1717-1797) arrived in Florence in 1739, together with the future poet THOMAS GRAY (1716-1771), on their Grand Tour. They had been close friends at Eton and at Cambridge, but their personalities were completely different and indeed their tour ended in bitterness and recrimination. Horace was the youngest son of the Prime Minister Sir Robert Walpole, and was very rich and spoilt and frivolous. Thomas Gray—who would be best known for his celebrated 'Elegy Written in a Country Churchyard'—was more studious and solemn, and was well aware that his expenses were being paid by Horace's father. They spent about nine months in France and Switzerland before crossing the Alps ('such uncouth rocks, and such uncomely inhabitants', noted Horace) and proceeding via Parma and Bologna to Florence. When they arrived they were most warmly greeted by Horace Mann, who was especially friendly to them because he owed his post to Horace Walpole's father Sir Robert.

The very next evening Mann presented them at an assembly of the Prince de Craon, Regent for the Grand Duke. Craon was head of the Regency Council, and at this time the Tuscan court swarmed with Lorrainers.

Both tourists were delighted by the acting British resident's friendliness and charm, and as we have seen Gray called him 'the best and most obliging person in the world.' He and Walpole spent their mornings exploring the streets, the churches, and especially the paintings assembled in the Palazzo Pitti and the wonderful collection of sculptures in 'the famous Gallery', the Uffizi. Before this neither of them had seen much classical sculpture: Gray had never seen the Arundelian collection at Oxford, for example, and he had probably not seen Sir Robert's collection of Italian paintings at Houghton. In Florence Gray studied the art in considerable detail and filled copious notebooks. As we might expect, he completely ignored the primitives and the art of the fifteenth century. He quite liked Raphael, Giorgione, Veronese and Titian, but he reserved his warmest praise for seventeenth-century painters such as Annibale Carracci, Domenichino, Guercino, Pietro da Cortona, Salvator Rosa, Carlo Maratti, and above all Guido Reni. Horace Walpole could not be bothered with Gray's notetaking. He too spent long hours in the Gallery, though he was far more interested in society and was becoming weary of the splendours of the past. 'I see several things that please me greatly', he wrote to his friend Richard West, 'but... I have left off screaming Lord! This, and Lord! That. To speak sincerely, Calais surprised me more than anything I have seen since.' He became the *cicisbeo* or *cavaliere servente* to Elisabetta Capponi, wife of the Marchese Grifoni, one of the most beautiful women in Florence, and she presented him with a white lapdog called Patapan. In Florence Walpole took rather a low view of his fellow countrymen, and late in January he wrote: 'The most remarkable thing I have observed since I came abroad is, that there are no people so obviously mad as the English.' But Horace was delighted by the Carnival early in 1740. Shrove Tuesday that year fell on 1 March. 'I have done nothing but slip out of my domino into bed, and out of bed into my domino. The end of the Carnival is frantic, bacchanalian; all the morn one makes parties to the shops and coffee-houses, and all the evening to the operas and balls. Then I have danced, good Gods! how I have danced.' When the blind Florentine pope Clement XII Corsini died in February, Walpole and Gray immediately set out for Rome in order to enjoy the ceremonies of the conclave. However, the cardinals took far too long to elect Clement's successor, so the pair of them decided—after a visit to Naples—to come back to Florence.

They settled into the Casa Ambrogi, from the windows of which it was possible to fish in the Arno (as they would both have known, Pliny the Younger was able to fish in lake Como from the windows of his Comedy

Horace Walpole

Villa, in the first century AD). Mann lived in the Casa Ambrogi himself, quite as much as in his official residence, which was the Casa Manetti on the south side of via Santo Spirito, at the corner of via Maffia. Again Mann was very agreeable; the climate was perfect; the summer days and nights drifted by in happy idleness. Florence, Gray told West, was 'an excellent place to employ all one's animal sensations in, but utterly contrary to one's rational powers.' He was fairly happy to accept the style of life that Horace Walpole found so agreeable: 'Here you shall get up at twelve o'clock, breakfast till three, dine till five, sleep till six, drink cooling liquors till eight, go to the bridge at ten, sup till two, and so sleep till twelve again.' After he left Florence Horace Walpole never saw Horace Mann again, though they continued to write to each other for over four decades on a scale truly phenomenal and, as Walpole remarked, 'not to be paralleled in the history of the post office.' The *Dictionary of National Biography* speculates that Walpole's hold over Mann was 'perhaps sexual', but in the absence of any evidence we cannot really say whether this was true or not. Walpole's brilliantly witty letters are among the finest in the English language, though unfortunately the same cannot be said for Mann's. Lord Dover, who published a selection of them in 1833, said they were 'voluminous, but particularly devoid of interest, as they are written in a dry heavy style, and consist almost entirely of trifling details of forgotten Florentine society.' (That is precisely why we like to read them.) In 1782, four years before his death, Mann was finally appointed Envoy Extraordinary and Plenipotentiary.

Gray made a collection of musical manuscripts, and began composing some Latin hexameters, but he too was having a good time, as he enjoyed watching the stream of life that flowed through the halls and salons of the palazzi, and along 'the charming bridge', the Ponte Santa Trìnita where everybody used to meet in the warm summer nights. All good things come to an end and it was soon time to go home. Shortly after leaving Florence, Walpole and Gray quarrelled, and they parted in anger. Gray seems to have been the touchier of the two, and he declined a reconciliation. They made their separate ways back to England.

Grand Tourists continued to arrive in Florence, generally accompanied by a travelling tutor or bear-leader. In the mid-1760s a bear-leader called William Patoun wrote an interesting MS entitled 'Advice on Travel in Italy', addressed to some unidentified noble patron. On the subject of accommodation in Florence he has this to say: 'There are two great lodging houses in Florence where the English usually go to, Vannini's and Charles's. Both equally good in all respects. Mrs Vannini is an English woman. Charles is protected greatly by Sir Horace Mann. The price of every article being fixed you will not be imposed on in any respect. Your Lordship will find the utmost attention paid to you by Sir Horace Mann. As your Lordship by this time will be pratico del paese I can say little relating to Florence that could be of Material Service. I need still less caution your Lordship against the contagion of indolence and dangling after the ladies, which prevails more at Florence than anywhere else.'

Tobias Smollett

The Scottish physician and novelist TOBIAS SMOLLETT (1721-1771; above) came to Florence early in 1765, mourning the death of his only child, a girl aged fifteen. On the way he and his wife Nancy were thrown from their carriage on the road from Arezzo, and were obliged to continue their journey on foot in pouring rain. They arrived at ten o'clock at night and went straight to the Widow Vannini's English inn, in what was then piazza Soderini and is now piazza Nazario Sauro. This was convenient for Smollett as it was just round the corner from Horace Mann's house in via Santo Spirito, which he visited often. He was back again in 1770, working on his amusing scatological novel *The Expedition of Humphrey Clinker*. It was Smollett who made the gnomic observation 'Some men are wise, and some are otherwise.' George Orwell called him 'Scotland's best novelist.' Smollett thought Italian women 'the most haughty, insolent, capricious and revengeful females on the face of the earth', and said he would rather 'be condemned for life to the gallies, than exercise the office of cicisbeo.' He was impressed by the splendour of the place: 'Florence is a noble city, that still retains all the marks of a majestic capital, such as piazzas, palaces, fountains, bridges, statues and arcades. I need not tell you that the churches here are magnificent, and adorned not only with pillars of oriental granite, porphyry, jasper, verde antico, and other precious stones; but also by capital pieces of painting by the most eminent masters.' He did however deplore the way that some of the churches (San Lorenzo, Santa Maria del Carmine, the Cestello, San Paolino, even Santa Croce and the Duomo at this date) had bald unfinished façades: 'Several of these churches... stand without fronts, for want of money to complete the plans.' In the Tribuna of the Uffizi, Smollett 'was most charmed with the Venus [of Urbino] by Titian, which has a sweetness of expression and tenderness of colouring not to be described.' Of the marble Roman boar, the ancestor of the more famous bronze one (the *porcellino* or piglet, in the Mercato Nuovo), Smollett wrote: 'There is a wild boar represented lying on one side, which I admire as a masterpiece. The savageness of his appearance is finely contrasted with the ease and indolence of the attitude. Were I to meet with a living boar lying with the same expression, I should be tempted to stroke his bristles.'

Smollett died at the Villa del Giardino at Antignano near Leghorn (Livorno), and is buried together with his wife in the Protestant cemetery.

The painter and caricaturist THOMAS PATCH (1725-1782) arrived hurriedly in 1755 from Rome, where he had been studying with the '*vedutista*' Claude-Joseph Vernet until he was caught up in a homosexual scandal, and set himself up in a few rooms in via Santo Spirito, opposite the Casa Manetti. He brought with him a letter of introduction to Horace Mann. Grand Ducal Tuscany provided a more liberal atmosphere than did papal Rome, or for that matter than Protestant England. Thinking of the term 'bugger' or 'sod', the bear-leader William Patoun warned his charges that 'A certain Mr Patch at Florence is a —.'

Patch was an early admirer of Masaccio, and made twenty-six engravings of the Carmine frescoes, which were of some use to the restorers after the disastrous fire of 1771. His intimate friendship with Horace Mann, on the opposite side of via Santo Spirito, earned him many commissions from English tourists, such as a *View of Piazza della Signoria* now in Plymouth. Patch painted views of Florence and made caricatures of all his friends, in the 1760s. One called *The Punch Party* shows a group

Thomas Patch

of English people in Florence being waited on by Charles Hatfield or Hadfield, a genial innkeeper from Manchester, shown holding aloft a bowl of steaming punch. Hatfield had a series of disasters when four of his children were murdered by a mentally deranged nurse, but four more of his children did survive and one of his daughters grew up to be the painter and educationalist Maria Cosway, who became for a while the mistress of Thomas Jefferson.

In February 1771 Horace Mann wrote to Horace Walpole about his friend Thomas Patch, rather hoping that the hyper-critical Horace would share his high opinion of Patch's work: 'I am glad you like Patch's performances. He is really a genius, and all his productions have merit… He left Rome many years ago on account of some indiscretion about religion.' (Here Mann is putting a somewhat generic construction on Patch's troubles with the Roman authorities.) 'I took much to him, and though he does not live in my house he is never out of it a whole day. He has an excellent turn for caricature…'. Mann goes on: 'He was always an adorer of the heads of Masaccio in the Carmine, and both drew them and engraved them himself, and well he did it in time, for about a fortnight ago the church was almost consumed by fire, and those paintings so damaged that I believe none remain[s] entire.' Luckily this was quite untrue.

Patch followed up his book on Masaccio with studies of Fra Bartolomeo and Giotto (both 1772), and of Ghiberti (1774).

In April 1782 Mann wrote to tell Walpole about the sad demise of Patch, having evidently forgotten that he had already told Walpole all about him. 'I have been employed in a very melancholy scene, that of assisting a very worthy man who was most friendly attached to me, Mr Patch, of whom you may have heard my nephew speak. He was attacked yesterday morning with an apoplexy in my house, but finding himself ill, he went across the street [via Santo Spirito] to his own house and threw himself upon his bed. I was sent for, but found him speechless. He languished for a few hours, and expired this morning.' Patch was only fifty-seven. The nephew he mentions is Horace Mann the Younger, who saw quite a lot of Walpole in London.

GEORGE CLAVERING-COWPER, 3rd Earl COWPER (1738-1789), arrived under his courtesy title of Lord Fordwich on 7 July 1759 on his Grand Tour. The Florentines could not pronounce his name so they called him *Milord Forbici*, or 'Lord Scissors'. After succeeding to his father's title he acquired the splendid Villa Palmieri, and remained in Florence for many years. He was a great friend of Horace Mann (whose post he coveted), and of the Grand Duke (who cuckolded him). Zoffany included him in his Tribune picture. He only visited England once, three years before his death, and apparently found it a disappointment: this so often happens when people go back to their country of origin after many years of living in Florence. Lord Cowper was not only a collector, commissioning pictures for example from Anton Raphael Mengs, whom he met in Rome in 1762, but was also a patron of science: he corresponded with Alessandro Volta, after whom volts are named. He was made a member of the Florentine Academy, and of the Accademia della Crusca, and he also loved music and had his own private orchestra at the Villa Palmieri where Handel's *Alexander's Feast* was performed. From Zoffany Lord Cowper bought Raphael's exquisite *Niccolini Madonna*, signed and dated 1508 and now in the National Gallery in Washington.

In 1774 Cowper met the pretty fifteen-year-old Hannah Gore, who

Johann Zoffany: the Gore Family with George, 3rd Earl Cowper

was in Florence with her parents, and fell for her. In a painting by Zoffany we see the whole Gore family making music, while Lord Cowper particularly admires young Hannah, who is about to burst into song; she is shown standing beneath a painting of Hymen, the Hellenistic god of marriage and conjugal love. Cowper followed the Gore family to Rome and pestered them into allowing him to marry her privately in Florence on 2 June the following year. To his cousin he had written: 'they are the worthiest people I know; the youngest of the daughters I like very much... I hear they have fifty thousand pounds apiece, which would [do] very well.' She bore him three sons, but the marriage soon became the focus of Anglo-Florentine gossip, one of the most poisonous in all Europe. Horace Mann no doubt sounded as though he were protesting too much when he insisted to the gossipy Horace Walpole that 'the Earl & Countess of Cowper live on the best terms together'. A tourist called Thomas Pelham noted that 'the invidious & scandalous Florentines suppose Lady Cowper's intimacy at the Palace to be criminal', and indeed

Cowper's appointment as Prince of the Holy Roman Empire (*Reichsfürst*) was widely regarded as compensation for his wife's liaison with the Grand Duke Pietro Leopoldo, brother of the emperor Joseph II. 'She is the most beautiful woman I ever saw', wrote Thomas Brand in 1784, but added that she was 'proud and capricious, & almost all the travellers of this season are disgusted with her.' (In eighteenth-century usage, 'disgusted' was much milder than it is today.) After her husband's death Hannah stayed on in Italy, seeing a good deal of her sister Emily, until her death in 1824. She lies buried in Leghorn.

In June 1764 EDWARD GIBBON (1737-1794) arrived in Florence with his friend William Guise, on their Grand Tour. Guise was Horace Mann's first cousin once removed, and Gibbon had met him in Lausanne. 'By the road of Bologna and the Apennine I at last reached Florence, where I reposed from June to September, during the heat of the summer months... At home I had taken some lessons of Italian; on the spot I read with a learned native the classics of the Tuscan idiom; but the shortness of my time, and the use of the French language, prevented my acquiring any facility of speaking; and I was a silent spectator in the conversations of our envoy, Sir Horace Mann, whose most serious business was that of entertaining the English at his hospitable table.' In another place Gibbon gives a more circumstantial account of his arrival in the city: 'We had been so badly provided with horses that we did not reach Florence till nine in the evening. We stopped at a certain Charles Hatfield's an innkeeper well known among the English who speak very well of him.' The next day the local English came to call on him. 'In the evening we drove to the Porta San Gallo. It is the general and boring rendezvous of the Florentine nobility who come there to take the air, or rather the dust.' In a few days they learned with the other English to prefer the park of the Cascine, 'a fine meadow surrounded by trees.' Horace Mann introduced the future Historian to Florentine society, and Gibbon received many invitations from notables such as the Contessa Acciaiuoli and members of the Antinori family. In his usual obliging fashion Mann secured tickets for Gibbon and Guise in the Regent's box for the famous riderless horserace along the Corso, held on the feast of St Peter and St Paul and known as the Corsa dei Barbari. Gibbon relates that on hot evenings parties were held in the courtyards of the Florentine palazzi, which were

Edward Gibbon

beautifully lit up and hung with tapestries. Mann himself gave such a party in August which surpassed all the others: not only did the illuminations shine on the cream of Florentine society, but 'there were plenty of refreshments and the scene was enlivened by several French horns posted in the garden.' Gibbon paid no fewer than fourteen visits to the Uffizi, studying the antiquities with minute care. He soon realised that the celebrated antique statues had all been restored at various times, and made the prudent observation that 'the Writer is always afraid of building whole Systems based on the Caprice of some modern Sculptor.' In August he and William Guise went to call on Thomas Patch, but it would be too much to expect Gibbon to share Patch's enthusiasm for early Florentine painting and indeed he disapproved of the incorrect drawing of the primitives. After staying about three months he pressed on to Rome, the decline and fall of whose empire he was later to chronicle at such enormous length. Of course people still do come to Florence on their way to somewhere else, though they tend to stay here for very much less than three months, which seems a sensible amount of time to me. According to data, in 2016 the average tourist stayed in Florence for only 2.61 nights.

The diarist and future politician WILLIAM GUISE (1737-1783) met Edward Gibbon in Lausanne, and set off with him for Italy in 'great harmony and good humour' in April 1764. In a letter to his stepmother, Gibbon described Guise as 'a very sensible and well-bred man'; he also happened to be rather richer than Gibbon, and prepared to pay much of their expenses. They crossed the Alps together, Guise mounted on a mule and Gibbon, 'being no great Jockey', carried in a chair. They travelled via Turin, Milan, Genoa and Parma to Florence, arriving on Wednesday 20 June. At Charles Hatfield's inn they were charged 6 *paoli* a day for their large apartment overlooking the Arno. In the evening they paid their respects to Sir Horace Mann, who was a relation of Guise's. Guise began taking Italian lessons with 'the Abbey Pillory', Abate Antonio Pillori. Among the English tourists who were in Florence at this time were William Ponsonby, later 1st Baron Ponsonby; Henry Swinburne, future author of *Travels in the Two Sicilies*; Lord Fordwich, future 3rd Earl Cowper; Thomas Lyttelton, son of Lord Lyttelton, who 'seems to be a young man of parts, but very particular'.

On 29 June, the feast of St Peter and St Paul, as we have seen, Mann obtained tickets for Gibbon and Guise to attend the riderless horse race known as the Corsa dei Barbari. They very much enjoyed it. On the following day they went to a chariot race in piazza Santa Maria Novella, with four large chariots galloping around the two obelisks. Guise did not think much of it: 'This did not entertain us much, as I never saw much uglier Chariots, worse horses, or so bad conducted. The Prize was a piece of velvet, not worth much. Thus ended this famous Chariot race, much inferior to yesterday's in ev'ry respect.' At the Uffizi Guise listed the various rooms where the collections were displayed: Chambre des Peintres, Chambre des Porcelaines, Cabinet des Idols, Chambre des Arts, Chambre des Tableaux Flamands, Chambre de l'Hermaphrodite. In Guise's diary his remarks about the paintings are often perspicacious, and he was prepared to see the point of an early master like Fra Angelico: 'the painter that did them was by no means ignorant of his business', he thought, and the faces 'are far from being void of expression.'

Edward Gibbon crossing the Alps in a chair

Like Gibbon, Guise was rather bored by the evening assembly at the Porta San Gallo. He noted that the carriages would drive around for about a quarter of a mile, and that just before the Gate shut they would proceed to the Duomo, and remain there until the opera began. 'This is just the tiresome round we made this Evening, and many others, for want of having a better place to go, and to do like other people.' On 14 July Guise managed to catch a glimpse of Henry Stuart, Cardinal Duke of York, the brother of the 'Young Pretender', Charles Edward Stuart. The cardinal was staying at Palazzo Corsini just opposite Hatfield's inn. 'I could see plainly he looked very thin, unhealthy, and decay'd,' wrote Guise. On 26 July he gave a description of Titian's *Venus of Urbino*: 'Titian has here given to our view all the Charms of a most beautiful female figure, laying quite naked at full length on a white Bed... Her left arm is brought over her body, and with her left hand she prevents the modest Eye from being offended.' Guise and Gibbon saw a certain amount of young Lord Palmerston, whom they had known in Lausanne. He became the father of the future Prime Minister. In Palazzo Medici-Riccardi Guise was rightly impressed by the gallery upstairs: 'It is ritchly ornamented with gilding, and Glasses; The Ceiling from one end to the other is painted by Luca Giordano, in a very bold and beautiful manner. The figures, of which there are many, are Graceful, and natural, and the Colouring is bright, and strong, without being tawdry.' He does not however mention what is for most people today the principal attraction of the palazzo, the chapel with its fifteenth-century frescoes by Benozzo Gozzoli.

At San Lorenzo on 11 August he gave a description of the Chapel of the Princes, correctly pointing out that it was unlikely ever to be fin-ished: 'It is not very likely any future Prince, will think himself obliged to spend the sum, that would require; merely to compleating a pompous Mausoleum, for the Grandeur and Vanity of a Family that *formerly* was great.' On 16 August, as already mentioned, Guise and Gibbon visited Thomas Patch. They found him engaged on a large picture for the Duke of York, showing the Duke coming down the steps of Horace Mann's house, accompanied by Mann himself and a number of tourists, all caricatured. On 26 August Guise fell from his horse which rolled over his leg, 'hurting me more than I remember by any fall', so that he was lamed for some time. On 18 September Guise limped around looking for statues, 'of which there are many very good ones at Florence'. Of piazza della Signoria he wrote: 'Before the old Palace is a very large handsome Fountain in the middle of which is the Statue of Hercules [*recte* Neptune] of a Colossal Size, and round the fountain are a great number of smaller statues in Bronze, many of which appear to me very well executed. On one side of the Fountain is a very large Equestrian Statue [of Cosimo I, by Giambologna]. It does not appear to me to be remarkably beautiful, or perfect in any respect.' They left Florence on 22 September, and travelled via Lucca, Pisa, Leghorn, Siena and Viterbo to Rome. All in all Guise and Gibbon spent fourteen months together. They separated at Lyons, whence Gibbon returned to England, arriving late in June 1765. Guise got back a couple of months later. He succeeded to his father's baronetcy in 1769 and the following year became MP for Gloucestershire. He remained in Parliament for the rest of his life, though it appears that he only spoke twice in twelve years. (Gibbon amused his doctors with a parliamentary riddle: 'Why is a fat man like a Cornish borough? Because he never sees his member.')

In August 1765 the emperor Franz Stefan died, and within a month his third son appeared in Florence as the new Grand Duke, Pietro Leopoldo, aged eighteen. Pietro Leopoldo remained in Florence for twenty-five years, until he succeeded his brother Joseph on the imperial throne (as Leopold II). He was married to a daughter of Carlos III of Spain, Maria Luisa, and he put into effect a programme of 'enlightened reforms' throughout the Grand Duchy.

JOHN CHILD, 2nd Earl of TYLNEY (1712-1784), was one of Horace Mann's best and most useful friends. He was effete and very rich, and lived comfortably in Florence for fourteen years, in a pretty house near the Carmine which had a small garden where he kept 'a great quantity of golden pheasants.' Like Mann he was generous to the English visitors and allowed them to use his box at the theatre when he was away wintering in Naples. Lord Tylney had a wife and children, yet it was said that he was unable to 'resist the temptations & instigations of a passion, contrary to reason & at which nature shudders.' Lord Cowper remarked that Tylney's presence in Florence was 'a great resource' to Mann, for Tylney was regarded as the leading member of the Anglo-Florentine community, though people said that his 'understanding was not bright'. An unflattering vignette of Anglo-Florentine society, and of Lord Tylney's house near the Carmine, is provided by another celebrated Grand Tourist, the languid and supercilious William Beckford. Beckford has just given a rapturous description of the Boboli gardens. He continues: 'It was six o'clock, and all the world was going to my Lord T—'s, who lives in a fine house all over blue and silver, with stuffed birds, alabaster Cupids, and a thousand prettinesses more; but, after all, neither he nor his abode are worth mentioning. I found a deal of slopping and sipping of tea going forward, and many dawdlers assembled.'

In 1772 the German-born artist JOHAN ZOFFANY (1733-1810) arrived in Florence from London, with a commission to paint a picture of the Grand Ducal collections for King George III and Queen Charlotte. The royal couple had heard a good deal about the Grand Tour and Florence, and were very sorry that they would never be able to make the journey themselves. George was far too busy and Charlotte had sworn she would never again put to sea after her storm-tossed voyage to England when she nearly drowned. They admired Zoffany's carefully detailed interiors and hoped that he would paint for them a view of the Tribuna in the Uffizi, showing some of the Grand Duke's finest works of art. Zoffany arrived with royal letters of introduction and immediately set about rearranging the Tribuna to suit his taste, having various pictures and pieces of sculpture brought across the river from Palazzo Pitti, and generally making a nuisance of himself. He received every assistance from Sir Horace Mann and Lord Cowper and Thomas Patch, and he put them all into his painting, together with a great many English tourists who happened to be in Florence at the time. Prominently displayed in the foreground is Titian's *Venus of Urbino*.

There are some interesting remarks about the creation of the Tribuna picture in the letters of a young Grand Tourist, fresh from Eton and Christ Church, George Finch 9th Earl of Winchilsea. Early in 1773 he wrote to his mother Lady Charlotte Finch: '...I go every Morning into the Gallery which I admire more & more, I believe it is allowed to be one of the finest things in the world, the Tribune in particular is the most charming thing I ever saw, it is that that Zoffani is drawing the Picture of, which is really one of the Most laborious undertakings I ever saw. For he not only Copies a great many Pictures & Statues & the Room, which is a great deal to do, but even the Frames and... the small bronzes, the Table etc, to make it be a complete and exact representation of the Room, and besides that he is obliged to put several of the Pictures in perspective, and to make a distinction between the life & the heads in the pictures... When it is done it will be a very pretty thing and will give a very good Idea of the originals.' Young Lord Winchilsea (who later played an important role in the history of cricket) reported with great delight to his mother that Zoffany 'asked me *to be in* it which *I am* accordingly to be & have sat once already.' He can be seen on the left of the little group admiring the statue of the Venus de' Medici, his head just above Thomas Patch's. (Patch is pointing with his left hand to the buttocks of one of the *Wrestlers*.)

Zoffany's painting of the Tribuna, now in the Royal Collections in London, is an iconic image that is emblematic of the Grand Tour, and a striking and beautiful picture; so it comes as a surprise to learn that King George and Queen Charlotte, who awarded the commission to Zoffany,

Hester Lynch Thrale (Mrs Piozzi)

absolutely hated it. They were furious with the German artist for clutter-
ing up the Tribuna with nonentities whom they had never met and never
heard of. They banished the picture from their presence.

In 1784 Thomas Brand noted that 'Old Sir Horace still winks his para-
lytic Eye & repeats his wonted Stories', but by the following year Mann
was looking 'sick and old', according to Mrs Piozzi. She was the former
HESTER THRALE (née Salusbury, 1741-1821), whose portrait was painted by
Joshua Reynolds; she had been a great friend of Dr Johnson, but lost his
friendship when she married the violinist Gabriele Mario Piozzi in July
1784. The Piozzis at once set out for Florence (Dr Johnson died while
they were en route) and settled into the so-called English House inside
Palazzo Ricasoli in what is now piazza Goldoni. There they set up a little
'Academy', frequented by a not very good poet called Robert Merry, by
Mrs Robinson the actress, and by three writers called Adney, Parsons
and Greatheed. (The not very good poet was one of Lady Cowper's
many lovers.) In Florence Hester Piozzi wrote her *Anecdotes of the Late
Samuel Johnson* and contributed to a volume about the Academy called
The Florence Miscellany, which was widely read in England. Its tone was

self-congratulatory: 'Why we wrote the verses', Mrs Piozzi wrote, 'may be easily explain'd, we wrote them to divert ourselves, and to say kind things of each other; we collected them that our reciprocal expressions of kindness might not be lost; and we printed them because we had no need to be ashamed of our mutual partiality.'

Mrs Piozzi left Florence in the summer of 1786, and did so with regret: 'But I must bid adieu to beautiful Florence, where the streets are kept so clean one is afraid to dirty them, and not one's self, by walking in them: where the public walks are all nicely weeded, as in England, and the gardens have a homeish and Bath-like look, that is excessively cheering to an English eye.'

In 1771 Horace Mann received a visit from King George III's younger brother, Prince WILLIAM HENRY, Duke of GLOUCESTER AND EDINBURGH (1743-1805). He stayed at Charles Hatfield's inn on the lungarno, accompanied by his secret wife Lady Waldegrave, who was not yet acknowledged as being married to him. It was he, rather than his brother the king, who once remarked to Edward Gibbon: 'Another damn'd, thick, square book! Always scribble, scribble, scribble! Eh! Mr Gibbon?'

WILLIAM BECKFORD (1760-1844) arrived in September 1780 while working on his amusing spoof *Biographical Memoirs of Extraordinary Painters*, and stayed on the north side of the river, on the lungarno between the Ponte Vecchio and the Uffizi. It was Beckford who first said about Florence Cathedral—and his remark has been repeated many times—that 'The architect seems to have turned his building inside out: nothing in art is more ornamental than the exterior, and few churches are so simple within.' Beckford was immensely rich, having inherited a fortune founded on sugar production and slavery in the West Indies. His godfather was William Pitt the Elder. When he was five he was given music lessons by Mozart, who was nine. In Florence he enjoyed sightseeing, and examined the antiquities 'like a butterfly in a parterre', as he said. One of his letters has a good description of the Boboli Gardens in the 'picturesque' manner, an example of a kind of travel writing that had enormous appeal at the time: 'What a serene sky! what mellowness in the tints of the mountains! A purple haze concealed the bases, whilst their

William Beckford

summits were invested with saffron light, discovering every white cot and every copse that clothed their declivities. The prospect widened as I ascended the terraces of the garden. After traversing many long alleys, brown with impending foliage, I reached the opening on the brow of the hill, and seated myself under the statue of Ceres. I surveyed the mosaic cupolas of the Duomo, its quaint turret, and one still more grotesque in its neighbourhood, built not improbably in the style of ancient Etruria [a weird remark if he is referring to the Badia Fiorentina]. Beyond this singular group of buildings a plain stretches itself far and wide, scattered over with villas, gardens, and groves of pine and olive, quite to the feet of the mountains. After I had marked the sun's going down, I went through a plat of vines hanging on the steeps to a little eminence, round which the wood grows wilder and more luxuriant, and the cypresses shoot up to a surprising elevation. The pruners have spared this sylvan corner, and suffered the bays to put forth their branches, and the ilex to dangle over the walks, many of whose entrances are nearly over-grown.' In 1786 Beckford published his Gothick novel, *Vathek*, written in French. He purchased Gibbon's library of 6,000 books for £950. He lived to a great age, and built up his own birthplace Fonthill Abbey, with a spire taller than that of Salisbury Cathedral, and lived to see it all collapse. Beckford had driven his workers like slaves, and they had made inadequate foundations.

With the outbreak of the French Revolutionary Wars, the British were unable to travel abroad, and the Age of the Grand Tour—as well as a chapter in the history of the Anglo-Florentine community—came to an abrupt conclusion.

The Boboli Gardens in the 1920s

Florence, an illustration by JMW Turner for Samuel Rogers' Italy, ca 1826-7

II

THE EARLIER NINETEENTH CENTURY

PIETRO LEOPOLDO was succeeded as Grand Duke by Ferdinando III in 1790. Ferdinando sought to remain neutral in turbulent political times but was obliged by pressure from England to join the anti-revolutionary coalition. He was thrown out during the French Revolutionary Wars, and in the spring of 1799 a provisional Jacobin government was set up. The Grand Duchy was dissolved and the Kingdom of Etruria was instituted. In 1808 Etruria was annexed to France, and in the following year Napoleon's sister Elisa Bacciocchi was installed as ruler, with the title of Grand Duchess of Tuscany. These Napoleonic arrangements collapsed in 1814, and by the Congress of Vienna Ferdinando III returned to power. The restoration was sensibly conducted and the French legislation was not abrogated (apart from divorce). Many public works were undertaken. Ferdinando died of malaria in 1824 and was succeeded by his son Leopoldo II.

SAMUEL ROGERS (1763-1855) arrived in Florence in 1814, one year before the final defeat of Napoleon. Rogers was a banker and rather rich, so he put up at Schneiderff's Hotel near the Ponte alla Carraia, on the lungarno Guicciardini, the most expensive hotel in town, so much frequented by the English as to be known as the 'Locanda d'Inghilterra' (Lady Blessington complained of its 'perpetual bustle, and never-ending odour of soup'). He was entertained by all the local swells, Lord Holland, Lord Brownlow, the Countess of Albany. His conversation was bitter and sarcastic, but he excused himself by saying that he had such a small voice that nobody listened if he said pleasant things. Yet deep-down Rogers seems to have been benevolent; the actress Fanny Kemble said of him: 'He certainly had the kindest heart and unkindest tongue of anyone I ever knew.' A year after his arrival he announced: 'Florence has won my heart, and in Florence I should wish to live, beyond all the cities of the world.' He was back again in 1820. His long and not very good poem *Italy* was published anonymously in 1822, and six years later with his name attached to it, and it became a tremendous success. It has the lines:

> Of all the fairest Cities of the Earth
> None is so fair as Florence. 'Tis a gem
> Of purest ray; and what a light broke forth,
> When it emerged from darkness! Search within,
> Without; all is enchantment! 'Tis the Past
> Contending with the Present; and in turn
> Each has the mastery.

A sumptuous illustrated edition was published in 1830. 'Rome is sad, Naples is gay, but in Florence there is a cheerfulness, a classic elegance, that at once fills and gladdens the heart,' Rogers wrote. During his lifetime Rogers' literary reputation was extremely high, and he was famous for his literary breakfasts. His appearance was cadaverous, and he reminded people of a death's head.

WILLIAM WORDSWORTH (1770-1850) spent five months in Italy with his friend Henry Crabb Robinson, in the spring and summer of 1837, when the formerly radical but now conservative Lakeland poet was in his late sixties. He spent all of June and a week of July in Florence, staying in the house of Mesdames Certellini at no. 11 via della Vigna Nuova. This was an ideal base from which to explore the centre, being no distance at all from that renaissance masterpiece, the façade of Palazzo Rucellai. The weather was very hot. Wordsworth spoke Italian well and had made a study of the Italian poets while at University. In Florence he wrote two sonnets about Michelangelo, as well as one entitled 'Before the picture of the Baptist by Raphael', and one on 'Dante's Stone'. This is the so-called '*Sasso di Dante*' in piazza Duomo, where imaginative tourists like to lounge and feel themselves inspired by the Supreme Poet. Robinson persuaded Wordsworth to sit on it: 'I remember the pleasure he expressed,' wrote Robinson, 'when I said to him "You are now seated in Dante's chair".'

In the Tribuna of the Uffizi, Wordsworth fell asleep, sweetly oblivious of the Venus de' Medici and of the English tourists sniggering at him. He visited Vallombrosa, the 'shady valley' to the east of Florence, because it is mentioned in a beautiful simile in Milton's *Paradise Lost*. (It is however most unlikely that John Milton ever went to Vallombrosa when he was in Florence in 1638-1639, for it would have been a difficult journey with no obvious point to it; he could easily have come across the name 'Vallombrosa' in Ariosto's *Orlando Furioso*.) Wordsworth also went to the shrine of Laverna, and to the monastery and hermitage at Camaldoli, on which he composed three sonnets. He wished that he could have visited Tuscany earlier in his life, and said so repeatedly to Robinson.

Sir WALTER SCOTT (1771-1832) spent only one night in Florence, at the Hotel Schneiderff in what is now lungarno Guicciardini no. 21. (An inscription in the hallway records his flying visit, together with those of St Catherine of Siena, Raphael, Napoleon and Byron.) The eminent Scottish novelist had set sail on the frigate HMS *Barham*, a 50-gun third-rate ship of the line put at his disposal by the Admiralty, in October 1831. His health was poor and the voyage was intended to improve it. After visiting Malta and Naples, where he was rapturously received, he was hurried home overland by his companions, in the hope that he would not expire before arriving at Abbotsford. This hope was not disappointed, and Scott died in his own bed on 21 September 1832, aged sixty-one.

Lady CHARLOTTE BURY (née Campbell, 1775-1861) arrived in Florence with her children in September 1817. She was the daughter of the Duke of Argyll and had been lady-in-waiting to Caroline of Brunswick, Princess of Wales, so she brought letters of introduction that admitted her into noble Florentine society, such as the coterie of the Countess of Albany. Horace Walpole and Walter Scott both praised her; Lady Stafford wrote of her 'None so pretty as she is'; the Gothick novelist 'Monk' Lewis called her 'the high-born and fairest of Caledonia's daughters'; the US Founding Father Gouverneur Morris noted in his diary in 1795: 'Lady Charlotte has the mania of being admired, which will, I think, lead her far.' In the following year she married her kinsman Colonel John Campbell, and had two sons and six daughters. Colonel Campbell died in 1808. The poet Ugo Foscolo wrote: 'Her daughters are the most graceful and charming creatures ever modelled by the hand of nature and adorned by education.' Her third daughter, Harriet Charlotte Beaujolais Campbell, known as Beaujolais, wrote an intelligent and charming diary at the age of sixteen. They stayed first at Schneiderff's Hotel and then at a house inside the Torrigiani gardens. Lady Charlotte took an interest in the mountain shrines of Tuscany, and eventually published her long poem *The Three Great Sanctuaries of Tuscany: Vallombrosa, Camaldoli and Laverna* in 1833, under her married name of Bury (in 1818 she had married her son's tutor, the Revd Edward John Bury). She and her daughters left Florence at the end of August 1820.

The Warwickshire-born poet and prose writer WALTER SAVAGE LANDOR (1775-1864) first came to Florence with his family in 1821 and took an apartment in via della Scala. He lived in all sorts of rented places until in 1829 he bought the Villa Gherardesca, at San Domenico di Fiesole, where

Walter Savage Landor

he resided in some splendour. We gather that he had delicious olive oil from his estate. After quarrelling with his wife Julia he left the Villa in the hands of his son Arnold and decamped to England. He wrote lapidary poems and magnificent classical prose in his celebrated series of *Imaginary Conversations*. An interesting remark he once made could be applied to Samuel Rogers: 'When a writer is praised above his merits in his own times, he is certain of being estimated below them in times succeeding.' Landor really is a good writer, though he has always been underappreciated. In his little book *ABC of Reading* (1934) the American modernist poet Ezra Pound asked the questions 'Why isn't Walter Savage Landor more read?... Has England ever produced an all-round man of letters of equal stature?' Later in the same book Pound bracketed Landor with Chaucer and Shakespeare, a triumvirate to which he did not add a fourth. Indeed, Landor is a colossus straddling the eighteenth and the nineteenth century. No English writer is more classical, for he wrote with equal facility in Latin and in English, yet he had a fiery and Romantic sensibility. Here is the well-known lyric called 'Dying speech of an old philosopher':

> I strove with none, for none was worth my strife;
> Nature I loved, and next to Nature, Art.
> I warmed both hands before the fire of Life:
> It sinks, and I am ready to depart.

Slightly less well-known, but similarly lapidary in manner, are these lines:

> Poet! I like not mealy fruit: give me
> Freshness and crispness and solidity.
> Apples are none the better over-ripe,
> And prime buck-venison I prefer to tripe.

Many have noted the extreme contrast between the Olympian calm of Landor's literary style and his furious explosive temperament. Far from striving with none, he strove with everyone he came across. He flung his cook out of the window at the Villa Gherardesca, and he knocked the hat off the head of an Italian marquis, his landlord in via Pandolfini, who had neglected to remove it in his presence.

In Florence in 1821 Landor and his wife Julia initially took an apartment in the palace of a Count Palatine named Charles de Lootz (italianised as 'Lozzi') in via della Scala, not far from Santa Maria Novella. He paid a year's rent in advance. At first all went well, for landlord and tenant shared an interest in art, and Landor bought from de Lootz three paintings that had once belonged to Sir Horace Mann.

One evening however when Landor was entertaining a young English painter called Trajan Wallis, and they were talking together pleasantly on the balcony, the count called out from his window that he was a sick man and they were disturbing his sleep.

Landor was apoplectic with rage, and immediately issued a challenge. The very next day he wrote to the Grand Duke's secretary, Prince Rospigliosi, demanding the intervention of His Serene Highness. From Palazzo Pitti the prince replied that this was hardly a matter for the royal court, and referred him to the police commissioner for the Santa Maria Novella district. The result was that Landor wrote, in his best Italian, to the Presidente del Buon Governo:

'Signor Presidente, I have been advised by the Commissionary of Police to make Your Excellency acquainted with an offence against the laws and customs committed by a certain Lootz, who calls himself Count Lozzi... On Saturday evening from nine to ten, the painter Signor Wallis was paying me a visit. We were speaking of a painting of his, in the presence of my wife, on the terrace, 65 paces from the terrace of the said Lootz... A few minutes after ten, this Lootz cried out "Fine impertinence! to disturb people from slumber at this hour". He was not asleep—servants were passing in and out... I stepped forward, demanded an apology for the insult, and threatened the punishment he deserved... Three doctors a short time back swore that this Lootz was gravely ill. I, during the same period, have seen him running across the terrace like a small boy: during the same period he pinched the porter's daughter on the thigh and attempted other familiarities, as she told my servant; hardly a sick man! During the same period this invalid took into his service a young female very well known in the lobbies of the theatres. On Sunday he dared to show himself publicly in the Via dei Servi, fresh, lusty, laughing, in perfect confidence...'. The affair petered out in a series of compromises, but Landor was able to break his lease on the Palazzo Lozzi, which perhaps had been his aim all along.

In early November he took a new lease on one of the palazzi owned by the Marchese de' Medici-Tornaquinci, in the borgo degli Albizi not far from the Bargello. It was 'an immense palace, with warm and cold baths, and everything desirable'. Landor furnished fourteen rooms in his apartment at a cost of £600. His rent was under £50 a year (about £6,000 in modern money). A few months later there was another excitement when a chambermaid called Maria Santi brought criminal proceedings against 'Count Walter Savage Landor' for having poured boiling water over her, no doubt from the hot plumbing. The matter seems to have been settled out of court, but the police noted that Landor behaved 'with a maximum of scorn, insubordination and irreverence, to the point that he had to be called to order.'

In 1826 Landor took his family for the summer to the Villa Castiglione (now Lambertini) in via Chiantigiana on the south side of the river, situated on a vine-covered hill known as Poggio alla Mele, and in the autumn they returned to another palazzo owned by the Marchese Medici-Tornaquinci, in via Pandolfini, probably the house that is now no. 16, back-to-back with the one in the borgo degli Albizi. There he had a furious argument with a window cleaner called Bronchelli, and was sued for a trifling sum of money.

At Christmas that year Landor wrote to his mother: 'We are very gay here at Florence. Last night we were at a private play, given by Lord Normanby. He and Lady Normanby act admirably.'

One couple who especially enjoyed the Normanby amateur theatricals was the Earl and Countess of Blessington. Lady Blessington in particular was fond of literary society, and soon Landor was spending every evening at what she called her charming pavilion overlooking the Arno, at the Casa de' Pecori.

One evening at the Normanby theatricals Landor 'got into one of his moods of uproarious hilarity' in the interval between scenes. 'His stentorian laughter was still at its height when the next scene opened, Lord Normanby alone on the stage. Quite indifferent to, or unconscious of the impropriety, he continued deafening the house, while Lord Normanby, in the best possible humour, unable to contain his smiles, waited quite patiently until Landor had laughed himself out. Lord Normanby delighted in Landor.'

A little later the Earl of Blessington took Landor on his yacht, the *Bolivar* (once owned by Byron), for a short holiday in Naples, which city much delighted him: 'Those who have not seen it can form no idea of its beauty from anything they have seen elsewhere.' He loved the ruined Greek temples at Paestum, calling them 'magnificent'; 'but Grecian architecture does not turn into ruin so grandly as gothic', he observed. Back in Florence on his return from Naples, Landor became especially friendly with the Neapolitan Francesco Ricciardi, conte di Camaldoli, whom he thought far friendlier than the Florentines.

Just before the Landors moved out of the via Pandolfini apartment there occurred the already-mentioned incident of the marchese's hat, thus described by Seymour Kirkup: 'Mrs Landor was sitting in the drawing-room... where I and some others were, when the marquis came strutting in without removing his hat. But he had scarcely advanced three steps from the door when Landor walked up to him quickly and knocked his hat off, then took him by the arm and turned him out. You should have heard Landor's shout of laughter at his own anger when it was all over, inextinguishable laughter which none of us could resist.'

Landor and his family spent the winter of 1827-1828 in various Florentine lodgings, including the Casa Cremani at the Croce al Trebbio, where he violently kicked a carpenter named Giuseppe Pannucci and was reported

Interior of Palazzo Giugni-Fraschetti

to the police. Landor was obliged to foot the bill, but Giuseppe said he was tired of the ill treatment and would never work for Landor again.

While he was staying round the corner at the Casa Castellani in via dei Banchi, Landor had a fierce altercation with a picture framer called Natale Ussi, in whose shop he thought he spotted a painting that had been stolen from him. During the night a note was stuck on the door of Ussi's shop, warning the English that the owner was a thief: Ussi insisted that the handwriting was Landor's.

Eventually he settled into the Palazzo Giugni (now Palazzo Fraschetti, via degli Alfani, no. 48), an elegant Mannerist palace designed by Bartolommeo Ammannati that became the Landors' final Florentine home before they moved to Fiesole. In the spring of 1824 Landor suddenly found himself banished from his adoptive city.

What had happened was that he had dismissed a servant from Palazzo Giugni, and the man had retained the key and used it, so Landor thought, to gain admittance and steal some silver plate.

Next morning Landor reported the theft to the police, saying that he considered it his duty to do so, though of course he knew better than to expect the police to be of the slightest use, 'it being their policy when thefts are committed against foreigners to act so as to protect the thieves.' The officer on duty was naturally indignant at this offensive speech, and next morning Landor was ordered to be out of Tuscany within three days.

He appealed to the Grand Duke Leopoldo II, but in the meanwhile was obliged to leave Florence for the Bagni di Lucca, which at that time were outside the borders of Tuscany. Julia wrote to Palazzo Pitti: 'A wife distraught and afflicted makes this supplication: four tender and inno-cent Children pray and implore the recall to Florence of their respective Husband and Father.' Fortunately the Grand Duke took the whole matter good-humouredly, and gave orders that Landor should be allowed back to Florence. But did he learn his lesson and learn to bridle his tongue? He did not.

In August that year, with the help of a rich Welsh friend called Joseph Ablett, Landor purchased the Villa Gherardesca at San Domenico di Fiesole for 8,600 scudi from its owner Gatti, who had himself paid 6,400 for it less than two years previously. The property, now known as Villa La Torraccia, comprised some eighty-four acres, and there were 165 centu-ry-old lemon trees. It had historical and literary associations. Landor told Robert Sothey that his new purchase was a villa 'belonging to the Count Gherardesca, of the family of Count Ugolino, and on the spot where Boccaccio led his women to bathe when they had left the first scene of their story-telling. Here I shall pass my life: long or short, no matter.' His wanderings were now over for a while and he seems to have been relatively happy. He set about making a garden, having seeds sent to him from England.

At the Villa Gherardesca, Landor said, 'I have the best water, the best air and the best oil in the world. My country now is Italy, where I have residence for life, and literally may sit under my own vine and my own fig-tree.' (This is a reference to the Old Testament prophet Micheas: 'And every man shall sit under his own vine and his own fig-tree.') 'I have some thousands of the one and some scores of the other, with myrtles, pomegranates, gaggias and mimosas in great quantity.' Relative content-ment did not however make him less quarrelsome, and before long he was engaged in an epic wrangle over water rights with his new neigh-bour, M. Joseph Antoir, a secretary and attaché at the French Legation. The case was in and out of the courts for a dozen years and was finally settled in 1842 at a cost to Landor of between £200 and £300. This dispute about water gave Charles Dickens the idea for the quarrel in *Bleak House* between Sir Leicester Dedlock and Lawrence Boythorn, who is an affectionate caricature of Landor.

Dickens, who was thirty-seven years younger than Landor, wrote of Boythorn: 'Talking, laughing or snoring, his lungs made the beams of the house shake.' And Landor wrote this complimentary little couplet: 'You ask me what I see in Dickens... / A game-cock among bantam chickens.'

The archaeologist Austen Henry Layard, who spent his childhood in Florence and later excavated Nimrud and Nineveh, provides us with a glimpse of Landor's family life. 'During these happy hours that passed on the Fiesole hills I frequently saw Mr Landor, who was always very kind to me... The strange life that he was leading, and his eccentric character and quarrelsome disposition, kept him aloof from the English residents at Florence, and neither he nor Mrs Landor came to our house... In bringing up his children he put into practice certain theories of his own.'

(After the birth of Arnold in Como, Julia was born in 1820, the second son Walter in 1822 and the third son Charles in 1825.) The four children, according to Layard, 'were allowed to run wild, nearly barefooted, and in peasant's dress among the contadini. Almost before they could lisp, he began to teach them ancient Greek. They were not sent to school'— Layard is wrong on this point, they did go to school in Florence—'and the only time at which they were subjected to any kind of discipline was when his ungovernable temper was excited by something which they may have done to displease him, when he treated them very harshly.' This obviously was not a good method of child-rearing, and it was no doubt responsible for many of the problems that later arose between Landor and his sons and daughter. He himself claimed that he loved all children: 'to see the happiness of children was always to me the first of all happiness', he said.

It was in Florence that Landor began and almost completed the series of *Imaginary Conversations* that are his chief claim to literary celebrity. They were published in five volumes between 1824 and 1829, others being added later. The idea of these dialogues had been conceived during Landor's childhood, as he later wrote: 'When I was younger... among the chief pleasures of my life, and among the commonest of my occupations was the bringing before me such heroes and heroines of antiquity, such poets and sages, such of the prosperous and unfortunate as most interested me... Engaging them in conversations best suited to their characters.'

The *Imaginary Conversations* are in prose, for Landor once remarked: 'Poetry was always my amusement, prose my study and business.' Indeed, the critic de Selincourt gave it as his opinion that 'As a writer of prose none has surpassed him.' The range of interlocutors is vast, and there are more than 150 of them.

Perhaps the most magnificent of all are the Greek dialogues, for Landor was steeped in the Hellenic world and his imagination responded ecstatically to the clear sunlight of Greece. There is a much-anthologised passage about death in the dialogue 'Aesop and Rhodope'. Aesop speaks: 'Laodaemia died; Helen died; Leda, the beloved of Jupiter, went before. It is better to repose in the earth betimes than to sit up late; better, than to cling pertinaciously to what we feel crumbling under us, and to protract an inevitable fall. We may enjoy the present, while we are insensible of infirmity and decay; but the present, like a note in music, is nothing but as it appertains to what is past and what is to come. There are no fields of amaranth on this side of the grave; there are no voices, O Rhodope, that are not soon mute, however tuneful; there is no name, with whatever emphasis of passionate love repeated, of which the echo is not faint at last.'

In one of the Roman conversations, a speaker says: 'We cannot conquer fate and necessity, yet we can yield to them in such a way as to be greater than if we could.'

And here is a passage from 'Pericles and Aspasia': 'There is a gloom in deep love, as in deep water: there is a silence in it which suspends the foot, and the folded arms and the dejected head are the images it reflects. No voice shakes its surface: the Muses themselves approach it with a tardy and a timid step, and with a low and tremulous and melancholy song.' The critic Rostrevor Hamilton comments on this passage: 'No one but Landor has drawn from the English language an effect of this kind, suggesting in its serenity and amplitude an Elysian repose. It requires the utmost delicacy to harmonise a quality so static and remote with the stir of human emotion. The beauty must not be flaunted: the elaboration must not be carried too far.'

Another prose work, the *Pentameron*, appeared in 1837. 'Some of the pages are too delicious to turn over', said Elizabeth Browning.

Here is a passage in which Giovanni Boccaccio recalls a dream that he has had: 'My dream expanded and moved forward. I trod again the dust of Posillipo, soft as the feathers in the wings of Sleep. I emerged on Baia; I crossed her innumerable arches; I loitered in the breezy sunshine of her mole; I trusted the faithful seclusion of her caverns, the keepers of so many secrets; and I reposed on the buoyancy of her tepid sea. Then Naples and her theatres and her churches, the grottos and dells and forts and promontories, rushed forward in confusion, now among soft whispers, now among sweetest sounds, and subsided, and sank, and disappeared. Yet a memory seemed to come fresh from every one: each had time enough for its tale, for its pleasure, for its reflection, for its pang.'

In March 1835 Landor's friend Charles Armitage Brown came to dinner at the Villa Gherardesca, and witnessed a painful altercation between Mr and Mrs Landor that effectively put an end to their marriage. When the couple separated, Landor was sixty and his wife Julia was forty-four. He returned to England and remained there for twenty-three years. Very correctly and gallantly he made over the villa to his wife and children. What brought him back to Italy, in 1858, was a most unfortunate libel action. That year he published a metrical miscellany entitled *Dry Sticks Faggotted by W.S. Landor*, in which he libelled two tiresome and disagreeable women who had behaved most ungratefully towards him. The verdict went against him and he was vilified in the press. The violence of the newspapers' language against the eighty-three-year-old culprit is quite astonishing. The *Saturday Review*, for instance: 'Filth and obscenity are never so unnaturally nauseous as from the chattering lips of age, and a tottering and toothless satyr generally keeps his foul life and conversation to himself and his associates', etc.. No wonder Landor decided to leave England for Italy.

At the Villa Gherardesca, however, he was coldly received by his wife and family, and his biographers all make the comparison with King Lear and his horribly ungrateful elder daughters. He spent ten miserable months at the villa, escaping several times but always being brought back.

Eventually he was found by Robert Browning, prowling the streets of Florence like a dishevelled lion, with no money at all. Browning took the old man back to Casa Guidi and set about securing an allowance from Landor's family in England. He then installed Landor in a cottage at Marciano outside Siena, where he was well looked after by the American sculptor William Wetmore Story and his family. There he was visited by Elizabeth Browning and Isa Blagden, and by the young American journalist Kate Field, who had an abundance of auburn hair, turquoise eyes and a milk-and-roses complexion. Landor fell for her at once and began giving her Latin lessons.

The Brownings' long-term plan, which they successfully and very kindly carried out, was to install Landor in Florence in the care of their faithful maid Wilson, who had followed them to Italy from Wimpole Street at the time of their famous elopement in 1846. Since then she had married an Italian, Ferdinando Romagnoli, and was living in via Nunziatina, a few hundred metres from Casa Guidi. Wilson and her husband had the ground floor and Landor was given three small rooms and a book closet on the first floor. The rent was £1 a week and Wilson was to be paid £30 a year for looking after him.

The street is now called via della Chiesa and the house is just opposite the Albergo Popolare, where drunks and homeless people are given shelter for the night. It was in this little house in via della Chiesa, not far from piazza Tasso, that Landor spent the remaining years of his life.

On one occasion Landor rang for Mrs Romagnoli at two o'clock in the morning, asking for windows to be thrown open, and for pen, ink and paper. Having written a few lines he leaned back and said 'I shall never write again. Put out the lights and draw the curtains.'

Yet he was not to be trifled with. Many years before, as is well known, he had thrown his cook out of the window at the Villa Gherardesca. To show that 'the old volcanic fire still lived beneath its ashes', Tom Trollope cited another defenestration episode, from this later period, in which Landor, having finished dinner, 'thinking that the servant did not come to remove the things so promptly as she ought to have done', gathered everything up in the tablecloth and bundled it out of the window.

In mid-September Landor had such a bad cold and a cough that he stayed in bed, something he never normally did. He had not eaten for three days when his younger sons Walter and Charles arrived separately to visit him on Saturday the 17th. Landor said he would take a pill for his cough, then changed his mind, then tried to take a drink, then laid down his head and died. He had written:

> Death stands above me, whispering low
> I know not what into my ear:
> Of his strange language all I know
> Is, there is not a word of fear.

William Hazlitt

He was buried in the Protestant cemetery outside Porta a Pinti, in what is now piazzale Donatello. The funeral was conducted by the Revd I.H.S. Pendleton, the Anglican chaplain. Only Landor's two younger sons were in attendance.

Of his own literary reputation, he had prophesied: 'I shall dine late, but the dining-room will be well lighted, the guests few and select.' Landor was the intemperate champion of temperance, the furious defender of serenity and sweet reasonableness.

The essayist and journalist WILLIAM HAZLITT (1778-1830) arrived by coach early in 1825, just in time for the Carnival, which that year ended on 15 February. He was under contract with *The London Morning Chronicle* to write a series of articles about Florence. At first he stayed in the fashionable Albergo delle Quattro Nazioni, in the Palazzo Gianfigliazzi on the lungarno Corsini (where the novelist Alessandro Manzoni was to stay, just two years later), but then he moved to some apartments in an 'English house' where he had every comfort except for heating. Hazlitt suffered a good deal from the cold, finding it difficult to write with numb fingers; but he said that in Florence, in a strange way, personal suffering did not diminish one's happiness. He saw a certain amount of Walter

Savage Landor, and went to visit Leigh Hunt at Villa Morandi and Charles Armitage Brown at Villa San Baldassarre, both at Maiano. Hazlitt thought that the modern buildings in Florence harmonised very well with the old ones, and in general that everything was very well preserved: 'The climate has been kind to the buildings', he said. He did not think much of Michelangelo's *David*: 'The David is as if a large mass of solid marble fell upon one's head, to crush one's faith in great names. It looks like an awkward overgrown actor at one of our minor theatres, without his clothes: the head is too big for the body, and it has a helpless expression of distress.' Hazlitt wrote amusingly about Raphael's *La Fornarina* ('you see her bosom swelling like the dough rising in the oven'): 'The Fornarina is a bouncing, buxom, sullen, saucy baker's daughter.' In Florence he observed that 'Many of the narrower streets are like lofty paved courts, cut through a solid quarry of stone. In general, the public buildings are old, and striking chiefly from their massiveness and the quaintness of the style and ornaments. Florence is like a town that has survived itself. It is distinguished by the remains of early and rude grandeur; it is left where it was three hundred years ago. Its history does not seem to be brought down to the present period.' Hazlitt's glowing descriptions of the city published in *The London Morning Chronicle* fired people's interest and made them long to come and see Florence for themselves.

FRANCES TROLLOPE (née Milton, 1780-1863) settled in Florence in the autumn of 1843 with her eldest son Tom, eleven years after the publication of her celebrated book *Domestic Manners of the Americans*. (As for the Americans' manners, she did not think highly of them: 'The total want of all the usual courtesies of the table, the voracious rapidity with which the viands were seized and devoured, the strange uncouth phrases and pronunciation; the loathsome spitting, from the contamination of which it was absolutely impossible to protect our dresses; the frightful manner of feeding with their knives, till the whole blade seemed to enter into the mouth; and the still more frightful manner of cleaning the teeth afterwards with a pocket knife, soon forced us to feel... that the dinner hour was to be any thing rather than an hour of enjoyment.') Mrs Trollope was an extremely voluminous writer, and she published 114 books, all written after her fiftieth birthday; if we add the books written by her two sons, we arrive at a total of over 300. She lived first in an apartment in Palazzo Passerini in via de' Bardi, then in Palazzo Dufour-Berte ('Casa Berti') in via Malcontenti. The beautiful garden and spacious rooms were well suited to the entertaining she went in for. Her salon was a rival to that of the Brownings, and attracted all sorts of people. In 1848 the family moved into the Villino on piazza Maria Antonia (for which see the entry on Anthony Trollope).

The London-born poet, critic and essayist LEIGH HUNT (1784-1859) came with his wife Marianne and their six children to Florence from Genoa in the summer of 1823, staying for a short time at no. 1 via delle Belle Donne, 'a name which it is a sort of tune to pronounce.' He had liked Genoa, but preferred Florence, where there were 'more conveniences for us, more books, more fine arts, more illustrious memories, and a greater concourse of Englishmen; so that we might possess, as it were, England and Italy together.' According to the publisher George Smith, 'Leigh Hunt was of a small stature, with sallow not to say yellow complexion.' It was Shelley who supported Hunt financially and who suggested that he might like to come to Florence. Next he lived on the first floor of the house at the corner of piazza Santa Croce and via Magliabecchi. Finally he moved to Maiano, to the Villa Morandi, which was close to where his friend Charles Armitage Brown resided at Villa San Baldassarre. Hunt showed Landor a single hair from the locks of Lucrezia Borgia, stolen for Hunt by a 'mad acquaintance' (possibly Byron) from the Ambrosian Library in Milan. Landor produced a pair of couplets:

Leigh Hunt

Borgia, thou once wert almost too august
And high for adoration; now thou'rt dust.
All that remains of thee these plaits unfold,
Calm hair, meandering in pellucid gold.

Hunt began writing articles on Florence and other topics for *The Examiner* and *The New Monthly Magazine*. He had a plan, suggested to him by Shelley and Byron, to bring out a quarterly journal for the English residents of Florence (who in 1825 comprised about 200 families), and went as far as getting permission from the authorities for it. However, there were difficulties: the censors could not read English, and they refused to accept Hunt's excellent translations into Italian. Disappointed by the failure of this project, he left Florence in September 1825. Shelley had drowned a week after Hunt's arrival in Italy, and Byron was by no means interested in supplying Hunt with funds: he seems to have regarded Hunt, as he regarded Keats, as a vulgar little Cockney beneath his notice. 'I loved Florence,' Leigh Hunt wrote, 'and saw nothing in it but cheerfulness and elegance. I loved the name, I loved the fine arts and old palaces.'

Leigh Hunt's friend CHARLES ARMITAGE BROWN (1786-1842) came to Florence in 1822, shortly after the death of his great friend John Keats. He brought with him his small son Carlino, to whom he was devoted. They settled in the former convent of San Baldassarre at Maiano, which was owned by the Rosselli del Turco family and had been converted into a private residence. Brown spoke Italian well. His friends included Walter Savage Landor, Edward Trelawny and Seymour Kirkup. From 1823 to 1825 he had as his neighbour Leigh Hunt, at the nearby Villa Morandi. Brown made notes for a biography of Keats but passed them on to Richard Monckton Milnes, whom he met in Florence: in 1848 Monckton Milnes published his *Life and Letters of Keats* to great acclaim. Edward Trelawny came to stay with Brown at San Baldassarre in 1829. In March 1835 Brown went to dinner at Landor's Villa Gherardesca, where two of the Landor children, Arnold and young Julia, were present. During the dinner Mrs Landor reproached her husband for something he had done, and as she talked the reproach became a more general attack upon his character.

It was not the first time that Brown had heard Julia Landor blaming her husband, but on this occasion she became hysterical. She poured out her heart in language that Brown found shameful to recall and painful to hear for what seemed to him about an hour. Landor sat composed and silent, until she seemed exhausted, when he said: 'I beg, madam, you will, if you think proper, proceed; as I made up my mind, from the first, to endure at least twice as much as you have been pleased yet to speak.' Strangely enough the meal seems to have continued around them, but when Mrs Landor at last withdrew from the dining-room Brown followed and remonstrated with her. This altercation was more than Landor could bear, and he moved out of the villa and into Florence. It was the end of their marriage. That same month Brown and his son left Florence for England: they later emigrated to New Zealand, where Carlino enjoyed an eminent military and political career. He fought in the first and second Taranaki War, and sat in the New Zealand parliament. He died aged eighty-one, run over by a train.

SEYMOUR KIRKUP (1788-1880) came to Florence for his delicate health in 1818: the climate must have suited him, as like Samuel Rogers he lived to be ninety-two. He resided in the Casa Caruana at the south end of the Ponte Vecchio, 'on the hip of the bridge', as he used to say. Kirkup was apparently quite a good painter but gave up painting around 1835 and devoted himself to collecting. He was eccentric and learned and surrounded himself with curious objects, and so he was much sought out by all English and American visitors. He had missed Keats's funeral in Rome in 1821 because he was ill in bed, but the following year he had been with Byron and Trelawny at the burning of Shelley's body on the beach near Viareggio. Kirkup bought Shelley's sofa at considerable expense, and used to lie on it hoping to be visited by the poet's ghost. Together with the American Richard Henry Wilde he discovered Dante's portrait in the chapel of the Bargello. 'Kirkup's library was famous for its unique collection of ancient books on magic and the black arts, of which he was an ardent student', wrote Austen Henry Layard, the discoverer of Nineveh and Babylon, who grew up in Florence. All visitors to the Tuscan capital dropped in on Kirkup, though 'after the death of his two favourite Spaniels, which warned him by their barking when visitors knocked or rang at his door, it was not easy... to get in.' The house had once been the headquarters of the Knights Templar, and Ariosto had lived there; unfortunately it was blown up in 1944. 'The two rooms which [Kirkup] inhabited during the day, and the one in which he slept, were strewn and choked with manuscripts, books, pictures, portfolios containing rare prints and original drawings, armour, tapestries... covered with a thick coat of dust.' Sitting like a goblin among his accumulated possessions, Seymour Kirkup made an indelible impression on all his visitors. 'When he sallied forth in his battered felt hat to a neighbouring café, where he had his simple meals, the street boys pointed to him as the *stregone*, the magician.' Kirkup was rather credulous and was taken in by a pair of pretty sisters, one of whom pretended to be a medium, and at the age of almost eighty was made to acknowledge the paternity of a baby called Imogen. When he was eighty-seven one of the sisters persuaded him to marry her. Eventually he was compelled to leave his beloved Florence for Leghorn, where one of the girls had a lover, and there he died in 1880. Nathaniel Hawthorne was evidently thinking about Kirkup when he wrote in *The Marble Faun*: '"Ah, I have seen him at Florence," observed Kenyon. "He is a necromancer, as you say, and dwells in an old mansion of the Knights Templars, close by the Ponte Vecchio, with a great many ghostly books, pictures, and antiquities, to make the house gloomy, and one bright-eyed little girl, to keep it cheerful!"'

Lord BYRON (1788-1824) spent very little time in Florence: only one day on his first visit in 1816, and only a few days, in the company of Samuel Rogers, on his second visit five years later. But he was quite certain he had no wish to live there. Rather snobbishly, he intensely disliked the English tourists: 'Florence and Naples are their Margate and Ramsgate, and much the same company too, by all accounts', he wrote to his Irish friend Thomas Moore.

JAMES FENIMORE COOPER (1789-1863) arrived from New York in October 1828, and approached the city from the north by carriage: 'The city of Florence appeared, seated on a plain, at the foot of the hills, with the dome of its cathedral starting out of the field of roofs, like a balloon about

James Fennimore Cooper

to ascend.' After a brief stay at the Hotel York on via Cerretani he took a large and well furnished apartment in the Palazzo Ricasoli in via del Cocomero, now via Ricasoli (or possibly in the other Palazzo Ricasoli in what is now piazza Goldoni). He was accompanied by his wife Susan Augusta, four daughters, a son and a nephew. By this time he had already written *The Last of the Mohicans* (1826) and the other four Leatherstocking tales. He had inherited a fortune from his father and came to Europe with his wife in the hopes of making even more money and of educating their children. Cooper made friends with the Swiss-born booklover Gian Pietro Vieusseux, and frequented his reading-room. He enjoyed Florence very much, and was presented at the Grand Ducal court. In the spring of 1829 he moved to Villa Sant'Ilario on via Sant'Ilario outside Porta Romana, which had beautiful views: 'Among other recommendations, it has two covered belvederes where one can sit in the breeze and over-look the groves of olive trees, with all the crowded objects of an Italian landscape.' In 1833 Cooper returned with his family to the United States, and published his *A Letter to my Countrymen*. In it he strongly urged that America should develop her own art and literature, ignoring the aristo-cratically tainted culture of Europe.

Marguerite, Countess of Blessington

MARGUERITE GARDINER, Countess of BLESSINGTON (née Power, 1789-1849), came with her husband the Earl in 1823 on their way to Naples, and stayed for a month. They were back again in the early spring of 1826. They took part in the amateur theatricals organised by Lord Mulgrave, the future Lord Normanby, which so amused Landor. In the Casa de' Pecori on the lungarno she held a sparkling salon (said to be second only to that of Madame de Staël), and was herself most sparkling. Augustus Hare the Elder wrote of her: 'She is attentive, she is clever, she is affable, she is amusing, she is Irish, she has black hair.' In her book *Idler in Italy*, published in 1839, she was highly complimentary about Landor: 'There is a natural dignity which appertains to him, that suits perfectly with the style of his conversation and his general appearance.' Writing to his mother, Landor for his part praised Lady Blessington as the most remarkable woman with whom he had ever conversed. Here she meditates on the Medici family of Florence: 'Through the streets which we now pass, paced many a brave and many a dark spirit, "fit for treason, strategy and spoil"; and many a branch of that family, the catalogue of whose crimes, as given by the old historians, forms one of the darkest that ever made a reader shudder.' (In this passage Lady Blessington misquotes *The Merchant of Venice*: it should be 'stratagems'.) There is a superb portrait of her by Thomas Lawrence in the Wallace Collection.

Percy Bysshe Shelley

PERCY BYSSHE SHELLEY (1792-1822) belonged, together with Lord Byron and John Keats, to the second generation of English Romantic poets. Although—unlike Byron—he was not at all well known during his lifetime, Shelley's poetical reputation grew immensely after he drowned at the age of twenty-nine, and in the Victorian age he was one of the most highly esteemed of all English poets. Ethereal, bloodless, incantatory, humourless and shrill, Shelley's poetical voice is highly distinctive and still attracts readers today; and suitably enough it is a voice that has always appealed to the young.

However, we sometimes get the impression that Shelley's grasp on reality was not very firm. On Magdalen Bridge in Oxford he accosted a poor woman carrying a baby, and in Platonic mood he demanded: 'Will your baby tell us anything about pre-existence?' 'He cannot speak, Sir,' was the woman's extremely polite reply.

In March 1818 Shelley left England for the Continent, travelling with his second wife Mary Wollstonecraft Godwin and with his young friend Claire Clairmont, who was Mary's adoptive sister and had recently given birth to a child by Lord Byron. In France they paused at Lyons before crossing the Alps and visiting Milan, Como, Pisa and Leghorn. Claire sent on the infant Allegra to Byron in Venice. The three adults settled for a while at the Bagni di Lucca, and Shelley began working on his translation of Plato's Symposium. Very soon Claire announced that she missed her little daughter dreadfully, and proposed taking herself off to join Byron in Venice: Shelley at once offered to accompany her as far as Florence (which he had never seen), leaving his wife behind at the Bagni.

From Florence on 18 August Shelley wrote to Mary, setting down his impressions of his first sight of the Tuscan capital: 'Yesterday's journey, performed in a one-horse cabriolet almost without springs over a rough road was excessively fatiguing. Clare [sic: Shelley consistently mis-spelt her name] suffered most from it; for as to myself there are occasions in which fatigue seems a useful medicine—as I have felt no pain in my side—a most delightful respite—since I left you. The country was various & exceedingly beautiful. Sometimes there were those low cultivated lands, with their vine festoons, and large bunches of grapes just becoming purple—at others we passed between high mountains, crowned with some of the most majestic Gothic ruins I ever saw, which frowned from the bare precipice, or were half seen among the olive copses. As we approached Florence, the country became cultivated to a very high degree, the plain was filled with the most beautiful villas, & as far as the eye could reach, the mountains were covered with them; for the plains are bounded on all sides by blue & misty mountains. The vines are here trailed on low trellises of reeds interwoven into crosses to support them, and the grapes, now almost ripe, are exceedingly abundant. You everywhere meet those teams of beautiful white oxen, which are now labouring the little vine-divided fields with their Virgilian ploughs & carts. Florence itself, that is the Lung Arno (for I have seen no more), I think is the most beautiful city I ever saw... Domes & steeples rise on all sides & the cleanliness is remarkably great.—On the other side there are the foldings of the Vale of Arno above, first the hills of olive & vine, then the chestnut woods, & then the blue & misty pine forests which invest the aerial Apennines that fade in the distance.—I have seldom seen a city so lovely at first sight as Florence.'

A little over a year after this first visit, in October 1819, the Shelleys moved to the city and settled into the boarding house of Madame Merveilleux du Plantis in Palazzo Marini, in what is now via Valfonda, as Florence was considered the safest place for the delivery of Mary's baby. On

Mary Wollstonecraft Shelley

12 November Percy Florence was born, a 'small but pretty' child who was to live until 1889. It was while Shelley was staying in this house (destroyed during the Second World War) that he wrote his celebrated 'Ode to the West Wind', having seen in the gardens of the Cascine leaves blowing, 'Yellow, and pale, and black, and hectic red'. He tells us in a note: 'This poem was conceived and chiefly written in a wood that skirts the Arno near Florence, and on a day when the tempestuous wind, whose temperature is at once mild and animating, was collecting the vapours that pour down the autumnal rains.' Shelley worked on the final act of his Aeschylean drama *Prometheus Unbound*, and he assiduously frequented the Uffizi, as we learn from the memoir composed by his cousin Tom Medwin and published in 1833: 'Shelley, while at Florence, passed much of his time in the Gallery, where, after his severe mental labours, his imagination reposed and luxuriated among the divine creations of the Greeks. The Niobe, the Venus Anadyamine, the group of Bacchus and Ampelus, were the objects of his inexhaustible and insatiable admiration. He had made ample notes on the wonders of art in this Gallery, from which, on my leaving Pisa, he allowed me to make extracts, far surpassing in eloquence anything Winkelman [*recte* Winckelmann] has left on this subject.' In the same memoir, Medwin published a famous and beautiful description of the view from the Boboli gardens which Shelley had written in Florence. Like the equally celebrated

description of the same scene by William Beckford, Shelley's 'View from the Pitti Gardens' is a consummate exercise in the 'picturesque':

'You see below, Florence a smokeless city, its domes and spires occupying the vale; and beyond to the right the Apennines, whose base extends even to the walls, and whose summits were intersected by ashen-coloured clouds. The green vallies of these mountains, which gently unfold themselves upon the plain, and the intervening hills covered with vineyards and olive plantations are occupied by the villas which are as it were another city; a Babylon of palaces and gardens. In the midst of the picture rolls the Arno, now full with the winter rains, through woods, and bounded with the aerial snow and summits of the Lucchese Apennines. On the left a magnificent buttress of lofty craggy hills, overgrown with wilderness, juts out in many shapes over a lovely vale, and approaches the walls of the city. Cascini and Ville occupy the pinnacles and the abutments of those hills, over which is seen at intervals the ætherial mountain line hoary with snow and intersected by clouds. The vale below is covered with cypress groves whose obeliskine forms of intense green pierce the grey shadow of the wintry hill that overhangs them.—The cypresses too of the garden form a magnificent foreground of accumulated verdure; pyramids of dark leaves and shining cones rising out of a mass, beneath which were cut like caverns recesses which conducted into walks.—The Cathedral with its grey marble Campanile and the other domes and spires of Florence were at our feet.'

On 1 July 1822 Shelley and his friend Edward Williams sailed to Leghorn in Shelley's new boat the *Don Juan*, which had been specially built for him in Genoa. Shelley was in love with Williams's wife Jane. There they met Leigh Hunt and Byron, and held some discussions about a possible new journal, to be called *The Liberal*.

On 8 July Shelley, Williams and their cabin boy Charles Vivian set out from Leghorn, on course for Lerici. In a violent storm the overmasted *Don Juan* was wrecked, and all three members of the inexperienced crew were drowned. Ten days later Shelley's decomposing body was washed up at Viareggio, and was identified by Edward Trelawny from the clothing and from the copy of Keats's *Lamia* in the jacket pocket, folded back at 'The Eve of St Agnes'.

In the presence of Lord Byron, Trelawny and some others, Shelley's body was cremated on the beach near Viareggio. Trelawny wrote: 'The heat from the sun and fire was so intense that the atmosphere was tremulous and wavy.

The corpse fell open and the heart was laid bare. The frontal bone of the skull, where it had been struck with the mattock, fell off; and, as the back of the head rested on the red-hot bottom bars of the furnace, the brains literally seethed, bubbled, and boiled as in a cauldron, for a very long time.' Trelawny made a grab for the poet's heart, and in doing so severely burnt his hand. Lord Byron found the whole spectacle a bit too much, rather revolting in fact, and retired early. He swam out to his yacht, the *Bolivar*. Trelawny gave the heart to Leigh Hunt, who preserved it in spirits of wine and refused to hand it over to Mary. (Later he relented and gave it to her.)

Shelley's ashes were subsequently buried in the non-Catholic cemetery at the Testaccio in Rome, not far from the Pyramid of Cestius.

William Rossetti, the brother of Dante Gabriel Rossetti, recorded that in 1863 an aged sailor confessed on his deathbed to having been part of a gang of pirates who attacked Shelley and Williams, under the impression that Lord Byron was on board with a large sum of money. They had not meant to sink the *Don Juan*, but merely to ram her. Trelawny, it is said, believed this version of events.

After the death of his friend Shelley, the adventurer EDWARD TRELAWNY (1792-1881) first came to Florence on 10 May 1823, bringing with him his black servant and three dogs. He met a great many people, and corresponded with Mary Shelley and Claire Clairmont. Having found a home for the dogs, he left on 27 June to join Byron in Greece, where he married and fought in the Greek War of Independence. In mid-February 1829 Trelawny returned to Florence and went to stay with Charles Armitage Brown at the Villa San Baldassarre. There he began to write his autobiography, encouraged by his friends: 'Brown and Landor are spurring me on,' he wrote, 'and are reviewing it sheet by sheet'. In late July he moved into the centre of town because he was to be joined by his two daughters, Eliza from his first marriage and Zella from his second. Eliza died shortly afterwards, and the grief-stricken Trelawny moved with four-year-old Zella into the Villa Paradisino, on the steep street known as Erta Canina. He found a nurse for Zella and a couple of peasants to manage the tiny farm. He sometimes visited Charles Armitage Brown, and sometimes Lord and Lady Burghersh (the British diplomatic representative and his wife). Otherwise he did not socialise, but concentrated on his writing.

Edward Trelawny

Thomas Macauley

THOMAS BABINGTON MACAULAY (1st Baron MACAULAY, 1800-1859) arrived in Florence on 2 November 1838, and immediately enrolled at the Gabinetto Vieusseux, a reading-room well supplied with European newspapers and journals, which at that time was located in Palazzo Buondelmonti in piazza Santa Trìnita. He stayed at the Hotel Schneiderff on the lungarno Guicciardini: 'My rooms look into a court adorned with orange trees and marble statues.' Macaulay the 'dictionary-in-breeches' knew Italian well and wrote poems in that language. He tells us that he 'walked through some of the rooms in the Palazzo Pitti; greatly admiring a little painting by Raphael [of the Tetramorph] from Ezekiel': he added pompously that the picture was so fine it 'almost' reconciled him to seeing God the Father on canvas. At Santa Croce he thought the outside ugly and mean, for the present façade had not yet been put on; he considered that the inside, though architecturally undistinguished, was 'consecrated by the dust of some of the greatest men that ever lived'. He was back again in 1856, accompanied by his nephew George Otto Trevelyan, this time staying in the Hotel du Nord in the beautiful Palazzo Bartolini-Salimbeni, on piazza Santa Trìnita. Macaulay revisited the places that had enthralled him two decades previously, and by way of relaxation in the evening he read Alessandro Manzoni's *I Promessi Sposi*.

Beaujolais Campbell, Viscountess Tullamore

The diarist BEAUJOLAIS CAMPBELL (later Viscountess TULLAMORE, 1801-1848) travelled to Florence from London with her mother and sisters in the summer of 1817. She described the approach to the city, which they reached on Sunday 14 September: 'The road lays between large tracts of hilly plains which appear like a slightly agitated sea and which produce olives vines fig trees corn &c &c all mixed together. Nothing could look richer or more fertile. But the grapes are uncommonly small. Epicures however consider them as far superior to all others. Our heavy carriages... rolled quickly along the flat pavement of the Florentine streets and in a very little while we reached Schneiderf's Hotel Lung L'Arno. It is considered the best in Florence and certainly is very good but the expense is enormous.' After a few days they moved out of their expensive hotel into Casa Torrigiana near Porta Romana: 'After seeing many in what is considered the fashionable situation mamma fixed upon this one which though out of the way has the advantage of being situated in the middle of a large and really beautiful garden [the Torrigiani gardens].' Beaujolais wrote: 'The weather is still very hot therefore we sit all with green shutters shut to keep out the air which is the great secret of freshness'—indeed, English people in Italy often take a while to learn this important lesson. She described their daily routine: 'We get up about six and walk till breakfast at eight, dine at one. Mamma is dressed and at breakfast at nine and goes out in the carriage at ½ after nine, dines at three, lays down and either goes to the Cascine the public drive or to the Miss Berries. This public walk is fine and shady... The beau monde only go there about six therefore it is soon too dark to see any thing. This is a bad arrangement.' She did a certain amount of sightseeing, and her remarks on paintings and sculptures are frequently acute. In the Uffizi she saw 'a bust of Cosimo the first by Benvenuto Cellini. It is considered as a very estimable performance and certainly represents the wickedness of the man most perfectly.'

On 4 October Lady Charlotte and her eldest daughter were presented to the Grand Duke Ferdinando III in the nearby Palazzo Pitti. Beaujolais was most indignant at the vulgarity of her fellow countrymen: 'There are about twenty other English who have the impudence to present themselves at this court because it is foreign whereas in England they would not dare to show their noses.' Ferdinando spoke briefly to Lady Charlotte, saying that he was pleased that she would be in Florence for his daughter's wedding.

On the 25th Beaujolais wrote: 'To day that agreeable person Miss Berry took me out in the carriage. We went out by the Porta San Niccolo to the Chiesa al Monte [San Salvatore al Monte]... I had been struck by the view but Agnes [Berry] made me find out new beauties. We walked from there to the Chiesa delle porte sante [the basilica of San Miniato] which is at a little distance from it: the exterior is all made of various marbles in the style of the Cathedral and part of the interior towards the grand front altar is remarkably beautiful: it is most minutely enlayed with different marbles.' The whole family were extremely sad at the death in childbirth of Princess Charlotte (daughter of the Prince Regent) in November 1817, for like many of the British they had hoped that she would one day ascend the throne. Beaujolais thought that the untimely death of the twenty-one-year-old princess was 'an event which is perhaps the most melancholy and the most disastrous that could have taken place'. The diary ends with Lady Charlotte's dramatic and (to her children) unwelcome marriage to her son's tutor, the Revd Edward John Bury, by whom she was to have another daughter.

In 1821 Beaujolais married Charles Bury (no relation), Viscount Tullamore, in Florence. They had six children. She died in Naples in 1848, predeceasing her mother by some thirteen years.

The Boston-born essayist and philosopher RALPH WALDO EMERSON (1803-1882) came to Florence in 1832 and stayed at the Hotel Minerva in piazza Santa Maria Novella. He admired the Duomo: 'How like an archangel's tent is this great Cathedral of many-colored marble set down in the midst of the city and by its side its wonderful campanile!' The campanile he found 'a sort of poem in architecture'. The weather was unusually hot, but he enjoyed walking in the Cascine and the Boboli and retreating to his 'cool spacious rooms'. Like Macaulay he read Manzoni in order to improve his Italian, and each morning breakfasted at Doney's, the elegant café in via Tornabuoni that had opened in 1827. It was famous for its delicious sorbets, *pasticceria*, tarts and jams. In April 1833 Emerson wrote in his journal: 'It is pleasant to see how affectionately all the artists who have resided here a little speak of going home to Florence.' He dined with Walter Savage Landor: 'I found him noble and courteous, living in a cloud of pictures at his Villa Gherardesca, a fine house commanding a beautiful landscape. I had inferred from his books, or magnified from some anecdotes, an impression of Achillean wrath, an untameable petulance. I do not know whether the imputation were just or not, but certainly on this May day his courtesy veiled that haughty mind, and he was the most patient and gentle of hosts. He praised the beautiful cyclamen which grows all about Florence; he admired Washington; talked of Wordsworth, Byron, Massinger, Beaumont and Fletcher. To be sure, he is decided in his opinions, likes to surprise, and is well content to impress, if possible, his English whim upon the immutable past.' Emerson found Florence, with its 'spacious well furnished lodgings', far more comfortable to live in than either Rome or Naples. He rightly admired the 'elegant curve of the Ponte Santa Trinita', which is said to have been based by its architect Bartolomeo Ammannati on the curve of the tombs at San Lorenzo, drawn freehand by Michelangelo. It was Michelangelo that Emerson came back to study in 1838, eventually producing a book on the subject. On his next visit, in 1873, he was accompanied by his daughter Ellen and they stayed at the Hotel du Nord, in Palazzo Bartolini-Salimbeni in piazza Santa Trìnita. By this time he was losing his memory, and if he were asked how he felt would reply briskly 'Quite well; I have lost my mental faculties, but am perfectly well'.

Charles Lever

Nathaniel Hawthorne

The Salem-born novelist NATHANIEL HAWTHORNE (1804-1864) came to Florence from Rome with his wife Sophia and their three children, in late May 1858, eight years after the publication of *The Scarlet Letter*. He had just served as US consul in Liverpool, where he had been visited by Herman Melville returning from Florence. It may have been Melville who suggested Florence as a suitable temporary home. The Hawthorne family took a seventeen-room apartment at no. 36 via de' Serragli, the Casa del Bello. In the garden at the back, adjoining the Torrigiani gardens, Hawthorne worked on the MS of his fantastical-pastoral-historical novel 'The Marble Faun', which he had begun in Rome. He made friends with the Brownings, Seymour Kirkup and the sculptor Hiram Powers, whose studio was just opposite the Casa del Bello. Rightly he admired the stained glass in the Duomo, which many tourists overlook. To avoid the August heat the Hawthornes moved into the forty-room Villa Montauto in Bellosguardo, where he completed his novel: it was published in Boston in 1860 as *The Marble Faun, or, The Romance of Monte Beni*.

Of the Villa Montauto Hawthorne wrote in a letter: 'I like my present residence immensely. The house stands on a hill, overlooking Florence, and is big enough to quarter a regiment.' The rent was only $28 a month (about a thousand dollars in modern money). Each member of the family, including the servants, had a suite of rooms, and there were 'vast wildernesses of upper rooms into which we have never yet sent exploring expeditions.'

The Irish novelist CHARLES LEVER (1806-1872) settled in Florence with his wife Catherine in August 1847, having visited the principal cities in Italy, and stayed for some twenty years. According to Robert Browning, Lever had no trace of an Irish accent. He had written a great many comic novels. His first home in Florence was the Casa Standish on via San Leopoldo (now via Cavour), a house that was bombed during the last War; it had a small private theatre where he put on plays for his Italian and English friends. Lever stayed next at the Villa Capponi at Arcetri, with its secret sunken garden; then at Palazzo Ximenes-Panciatichi in borgo Pinti; and then at Villa San Leonardo in via San Leonardo. He liked to spend the summer months at the Bagni di Lucca, or else at San Terenzio on the gulf of La Spezia. At the Bagni he told Elizabeth Browning that he had eight horses and six servants, and had never lived so cheaply in his life. He remained in Tuscany until 1867, when he was appointed British Consul at Trieste. In making the appointment, Lord Derby wrote to him: 'Here is six hundred a year for doing nothing, and you are just the man to do it.'

ELIZABETH BROWNING (née Barrett, 1806-1861) arrived in April 1847 with her husband Robert, her Spaniel Flush and her maid Wilson. They were all very small. They lived first in via delle Belle Donne on the corner of piazza Santa Maria Novella, and then in furnished rooms in piazza Pitti while waiting for their future home 'Casa Guidi' to be made ready for them. Poor ROBERT BROWNING (1812-1889) expected to spend the rest of his life with an invalid: Elizabeth had had it drummed into her by her tyrannical old brute of a father that she was really sick and would never recover, and in addition her doctors had prescribed so much opium for her most minor ailments that she was seriously addicted. (When they met in London she was taking 40 drops of laudanum a day, which is a good deal.) During their courtship Robert had opposed the idea of settling in Florence because he thought the city was 'inhabited by hordes of vulgar and pushing English, parvenus who would have been inexorably excluded from polite society in England.' They went to Florence for a visit, and fell in love with the beauty and 'celestial cheapness' of the city, and made it their headquarters for the remaining years of their married life. Robert and Elizabeth settled in the Casa Guidi, as they called it, a smallish apartment in via Maggio near the Grand Ducal Palace. It has

The Brownings

a balcony overlooking the church of San Felice, on the other side of via Mazzetta, where Elizabeth famously heard a little child singing 'O bella, O bella libertà'. Here they held their miniature court, to a wide circle of intellectuals and arty and political types, and here the great romantic lovers lived in happily married bliss, together with Elizabeth's famous Spaniel Flush (whose life was written by no less a biographer than Virginia Woolf). She had been accompanied from Wimpole Street by her faithful maid Wilson, who blotted her copybook in Elizabeth's eyes by marrying an Italian. Elizabeth was ardently republican, though she welcomed Napoleon III as she felt that he would free Italy, and Tuscany in particular, where she was shocked by the feebleness of the Grand Duke Leopoldo II. 'He is made of the stuff of princes—faithless and ignoble', she wrote. Robert was somewhat less extreme politically than she, and he did not share her taste for mediums and spiritualism: after she was gone he published a satirical poem on the subject, 'Mr Sludge the Medium'. Elizabeth did not think much of the rival salon at Villino Trollope: 'Mrs Trollope has recommended her "public" mornings which we shrink away from. She "receives" every Saturday morning in the most heterogeneous way

The Drawing Room at Casa Guidi

possible.' In 1848 she wrote 'Casa Guidi Windows', to record her reaction to the exciting political events. After suffering a series of miscarriages she gave birth in that year to a boy, Pen: she dressed him in girly clothes, and allowed his hair to grow long. 'Florence is my chimney corner, where I can skulk and be happy', Elizabeth wrote in a letter. (Pen by the way grew up to be a balding, cigar-smoking, brandy-drinking womaniser.) In another letter she wrote: 'Florence is beautiful, as I have said before, and must say again and again, most beautiful. The river rushes through the midst of its palaces like a crystal arrow, and it is hard to tell, when you see all by the clear sunset, whether those churches, and houses, and windows, and bridges, and people walking, in the water or out of the water, are the real walls and windows, and bridges, and people, and churches.' They spent a writing holiday at the Bagni di Lucca, that gloomy spa town north of Lucca, in a sunless valley surrounded by chestnut woods, which for some reason has always appealed to the British. Altogether they stayed there thrice (Byron and Shelley had visited it, Charles Lever stayed there, and so did Ouida—she is buried in the Protestant cemetery there beneath a monument based on the one by Jacopo della Quercia to Ilaria del Carreto in Lucca Cathedral). Another place the Brownings liked to visit was Siena, and it was there that Elizabeth collapsed on hearing of the death of her hero Cavour, the Italian patriot and prime minister of Piedmont. Cavour's death, according to Elizabeth's friend William Wetmore Story, 'greatly affected her. She... wept many tears for him... This agitation undoubtedly weakened her, and perhaps was the last feather that broke her down.' She caught a chill and died in Robert's arms on 29 June 1861, in the same bed in Casa Guidi where she had earlier given birth to Pen, and Browning wrote to his brother George that a crowd of sobbing Italians followed her funeral cortège to piazzale Donatello, and the shops were shut, because everyone 'knew who she was—the greatest English poet of the day, writer of the sublimest poem ever penned by woman, and Italy's truest and dearest of friends.' The poem he is referring to here is her novel in verse, *Aurora Leigh*, about which opinions are divided: some find it the most distinguished poem written by a woman in the nineteenth century, others would rather have all their teeth pulled out than listen to one more line of it.

It was in 1860 that Robert, browsing in a flea-market in Florence, came across the vellum-bound volume of documents on the Franceschini murder trial of 1698 and bought it on the spot. Having diffidently offered it to various other poets, including Tennyson, as a suitable subject for a long poem, he finally got down to writing his own masterpiece, *The Ring and the Book*, which was published in four volumes between 1868 and 1869. After Elizabeth's death Robert took Pen to the barber and had all his ringlets shorn off. He then left Florence for good, taking Pen with him. When he died old and famous in 1889, he was buried in Westminster Abbey (and not in piazzale Donatello with his wife).

Meanwhile, on 27 April 1859 the Grand Duke Leopoldo II had 'gracefully but sadly departed the Pitti', never to return. For reasons of political expedience, Florence became the new capital of Italy on 3 February 1865. Vast properties belonging to the former Grand Ducal family or to the Church were taken over and converted to other uses. Huge numbers of civil servants descended on Florence from Turin, and the price of accommodation sky-rocketed. A large section of the old town centre was razed to the ground, and new buildings went up on an unprecedented scale.

The architect who presided over all this destructive activity, Giuseppe Poggi, at least had the good sense to leave the many city gates standing. On 3 February 1871 the capital was transferred to Rome.

The first visit of the American poet HENRY WADSWORTH LONGFELLOW (1807-1882) was in 1828, when he took lodgings in a building next to the Hotel Minerva on piazza Santa Maria Novella: 'In front of my parlour window was the venerable Gothic church of Santa Maria Novella, in whose gloomy aisles Boccaccio has placed the opening scene of the *Decamerone.*' Longfellow had been promised a position teaching languages at Bowdoin College in Maine, provided he took a trip to Europe at his own expense. He fell in love with old European culture and perfected his command of several languages. He later became professor of Italian at Harvard. After the death by fire of his second wife Frances, Longfellow set about studying and translating Dante. The members of his 'Dante Club' included Charles Eliot Norton, William Dean Howells and James Russel Lowell. His blank verse translation of the *Divine Comedy* came out in three volumes in 1865-1867; it still has its defenders, some regarding it as the most accomplished English version. During his second visit, from 1868 to 1869, Longfellow stayed at the Hotel Arno on the lungarno Acciaiuoli (destroyed in the Second World War). In 1874 he wrote a sonnet on the Ponte Vecchio, beginning with a misstatement:

> Taddeo Gaddi built me. I am old;
> Five centuries old. I plant my foot of stone
> Upon the Arno, as St Michael's own
> Was planted on the dragon. Fold by fold
> Beneath me as it struggles, I behold
> Its glistening scales...

(The true architect of the Ponte Vecchio is thought to have been Neri di Fioravante from Pistoia.)

The Lincolnshire poet ALFRED TENNYSON (1st Baron TENNYSON, 1809-1892) made several attempts in the 1840s to visit Italy, but found it difficult to

Henry Wadsworth Longfellow

Alfred, Lord Tennyson

tear himself away from England. His musical elder brother Frederick had studied the organ in Milan, and together with their brothers Arthur and Septimus settled in Italy. In 1839 Frederick married Maria Giuliotti and they had a son called Giulio, or Julius. When Wordsworth died in 1850, Alfred was appointed Poet Laureate. That year Frederick moved into the fifteenth-century Villa Torrigiani near Sesto Fiorentino (in what is now via Fratelli Rosselli in the hamlet of Quinto Alto). Alfred married that year, and in 1851 his infant son died. It was this sorrow that finally persuaded Alfred to leave England and join Frederick for a while at the Villa Torrigiani. On the way, he and his wife Emily spent three weeks at the Bagni di Lucca. There they rejoiced in 'the glorious violet colouring of the Apennines, and the picturesqueness of the peasants beating out their flax or spinning with their distaffs at their cottage doors.' In his memoir, Alfred's son Hallam wrote: 'Thence they journeyed to Florence to stay with my uncle Frederick at the Villa Torrigiani, which had been for many [recte a couple of] years his home. On September 24th they left Florence.' Wherever he went, Tennyson took with him his travelling library of his nine favourite books (Shakespeare, Milton, Homer, Virgil, Horace, Pindar, Theocritus, Dante and Goethe).

Margaret d'Ossoli

William Makepeace Thackery

The Massachusetts-born feminist and political activist MARGARET D'OS-
SOLI (née Fuller, 1810-1850) first came to Florence with the family of the
sculptor William Wetmore Story and lived in Casa Bazzachi, at the corner
of piazza Indipendenza and what was then via Apollonia. She married
the Marchese d'Ossoli, a friend of Giuseppe Mazzini's, and became a
devoted advocate of Italian liberty. Her husband was ten years younger
than she. They settled in Florence in October 1849, in an apartment at
the corner of via delle Oche and via del Campanile, where she enjoyed a
happy family life with her husband and their child Angelino. The Italian
patriot Giuseppe Mazzini described her as 'a woman of the rarest, for
her love and active sympathy for all that is beautiful, great and holy, and
therefore for our Italy.' She was friends with Mrs Browning and with
Horace Sumner. Family matters required her return to the United States,
so on 17 May 1850 the d'Ossolis set sail from Leghorn with their child, the
child's nurse Celeste Paolini and Mr Sumner, on the freighter *Elizabeth*.
In a violent storm the ship was wrecked off Fire Island, just outside New
York Harbor, and all five of them were drowned. The MS of Margaret's
novel was lost at sea.

The Calcutta-born English novelist WILLIAM MAKEPEACE THACKERAY (1811-1863) came to Florence early in 1854, with his two daughters, to stay with his Irish novelist friend Charles Lever, at the Villa San Leonardo. Lever introduced Thackeray to the club and café society that he himself found so congenial. They would lunch at three o'clock at the Luna restaurant, on the corner of via della Condotta and vicolo de' Cerchi, where the speciality was a sort of fish soup or bouillabaisse. Thackeray wrote a little poem which he called 'The Ballad of Bouillabaisse', inspired not by Luna's in Florence but by Terr's in Paris. It has these lines:

> This Bouillabaisse a noble dish is—
> A sort of soup or broth, or brew,
> Or hotchpotch of all sorts of fishes,
> That Greenwich never could outdo;
> Green herbs, red peppers, mussels, saffron,
> Soles, onions, garlic, roach, and dace:
> All these you eat at TERR'S tavern,
> In that one dish of Bouillabaisse.

CHARLES DICKENS (1812-1870) came to Italy in 1844. It was the comparative failure of his sixth novel *Martin Chuzzlewit* that made him decide in the spring of 1844 to cross the Channel and live abroad for a year or so, which he thought would be a good deal cheaper than staying in England. In preparation for the voyage both Dickens and his wife Catherine took lessons in Italian; he already spoke passable French. He purchased an old and shabby coach for £45, 'about the size of your library', as he told his friend John Forster.

The travelling party consisted of the 'Inimitable Boz', as he unselfconsciously called himself, his wife, his sister-in-law Georgina, the five Dickens children, a cook, two nurses and the guide Louis Roche, whom Dickens called his 'brave courier'. There was also a small white dog named Timber. The 'caravan' or 'menagerie', as he sometimes called it, crossed France, sailed from Marseille, and rumbled into Genoa on 16 July 1844. The house that had been booked for them turned out to be most unsuitable and full of fleas, so in September they moved into the Palazzo delle Peschiere, a fairly splendid villa that was built in 1560 for the nobleman Tobia Pallavicino and is still owned by the Pallavicino family. Before moving in, he had a water closet installed. With its 50-foot ceilings, it was by far the grandest house Dickens had ever lived in.

In November 1844 he nipped back to London, alone, in order to read his recently written story *The Chimes* to a circle of his friends. A famous drawing by Daniel Maclise shows Dickens, his head surrounded by rays of celestial light, reading the story aloud to a number of friends, all of whom are labelled. *The Chimes* is the second of Dickens's five Christmas stories, after *A Christmas Carol*, and he intended it as 'a blow for the poor'. His audience, we are told, alternately roared with laughter and wept buckets.

He was back at the Peschiere in Genoa before Christmas, and the family made a series of excursions to Parma, Modena, Bologna, Ferrara, Venice, Verona, Mantua and Milan. From January to April 1845 they toured southern Italy, partly by rail, leaving the children and Timber behind. Their route took them to Carrara, Pisa, Leghorn, Siena, Rome and Naples.

To his philanthropist friend Angela Burdett-Cootes Dickens wrote on 18 March 1845:

'In the mass, I like the common people of Italy very much—the Neapolitans least of all; the Romans next, for they are fierce and brutal... Florence I have not yet seen: intending to take it, next week, on my way back to Genoa. But of all places I <u>have</u> seen, I like Venice, Genoa and Verona most.

'The Bay of Genoa has charms, in my eyes, which the Bay of Naples wants. The city of Genoa is very picturesque and beautiful. And the house we live in, is really like a Palace in a Fairy Tale.'

(Incidentally the phrase 'Fairy tale' was invented by Dickens, as too were the words flummoxed, butter-fingers, rampage, boredom, tousled, footlights, confusingly, dustbin and messiness.)

After Naples they visited Mt Vesuvius, Paestum, Monte Cassino and Perugia. On the road from Perugia they had a slight setback, which Dickens described in his travelogue *Pictures from Italy*, published in 1846:

'Suddenly, there is a ringing sound among our horses. The driver stops them. Sinking in his saddle, and casting up his eyes to Heaven, he delivers this apostrophe: "Oh Jove omnipotent! here is a horse has lost his shoe!" Notwithstanding the tremendous nature of this accident, and the utterly forlorn look and gesture (impossible in anyone but an Italian Vetturino) with which it is announced, it is not long in being repaired by a mortal Farrier, by whose assistance we reach Castiglione the same night, and Arezzo next day…

'But, how much beauty of another kind is here, when, on a fair clear morning, we look, from the summit of a hill, on Florence! See where it lies before us in a sun-lighted valley, bright with the winding Arno, and shut in by swelling hills; its domes, and towers, and palaces, rising from the rich country in a glittering heap, and shining in the sun like gold!'

This passage seems to me a most wonderful evocation of the city's initial impact. It appears to owe something to Shakespeare's Sonnet xxxiii. Dickens continues:

'Magnificently stern and sombre are the streets of beautiful Florence; and the strong old piles of building make such heaps of shadow, on the ground and in the river, that there is another and a different city of rich forms and fancies, always lying at our feet.'

This is a fanciful notion of the city reflected in water, possibly more suited to Venice than to Florence.

'Prodigious palaces, constructed for defence, with small distrustful windows heavily barred, and walls of great thickness formed of huge masses of rough stone, frown, in their old sulky state, on every street.' *Distrustful windows* is an example of the hypallage or transferred epithet, for it is not the windows that are distrustful, but the Florentines who have had them made.

While he was in Florence, staying at the Grand Hotel Royal de l'Arno on lungarno Acciaiuoli (now destroyed), Dickens called at at least two houses frequented by the English: the Casa Berti in what is now via San Giuseppe, where Frances Trollope lived with her son Thomas Adolphus, and Palazzo del Pugliese in via de' Serragli, the home of Lord and Lady Holland. His visit to the Trollopes is recorded in Thomas Adolphus's autobiography, *What I Remember*, published in 1887:

'One morning in Casa Berti my mother was most agreeably surprised by a card brought in to her with "Mr and Mrs Charles Dickens" on it. We had been among his heartiest admirers from the early days of Pickwick. I don't think we had happened to see the Sketches by Boz... it was with the greatest curiosity and interest that we saw the creator of all this enjoyment enter in the flesh. We were at first disappointed and disposed to imagine that there must be some mistake! No! that is not the man who wrote Pickwick! What we saw was a dandified, pretty-boy-looking sort of figure, singularly young looking, I thought, with a slight flavour of the whipper-snapper genus of humanity.'

Charles Dickens

Trollope then quotes Thomas Carlyle, who also described Dickens's appearance at about this time:

'He is a fine little fellow—Boz—I think. Clear blue intelligent eyes, eyebrows that he arches amazingly, large, protrusive, rather loose mouth, a face of most extreme mobility, which he shuttles about—eyebrows, eyes, mouth and all—in a very singular manner when speaking.'

Contradicting Carlyle, Tom says that Dickens's eyes were not blue but hazel, and that he was not a little fellow but quite a robust one. He remarks on Dickens's laugh:

'His laugh was brimful of enjoyment. There was a peculiar humorous protest in it when recounting or hearing anything absurd, as who should say "'Pon my soul, this is too ridiculous!"'

Dickens became good friends with Tom and in later years frequently met him in London.

The other house that the Dickenses visited was Palazzo del Pugliese, also known as Palazzo Ferroni. Henry Edward Fox, 4th Baron Holland, succeeded to his father's title in 1840. He had joined the diplomatic service aged twenty-nine, and from 1839 until 1846 he was British Minister to the Grand Ducal court of Tuscany. He was married to Mary Augusta, daughter of the 8th Earl of Coventry. Like the earlier Minister Sir Horace Mann, Lord Holland entertained English visitors in his home, Palazzo del Pugliese, a huge building on the corner of via de' Serragli and borgo San Frediano. Tom Trollope thought Lord Holland 'one of the most amusing talkers I ever knew.' John Ruskin dined with him on 12 June 1845, and superciliously described him as 'a little of the exquisite, but I daresay amiable enough in his way.' Ruskin did however admire the house: 'Nice cool rooms after dinner, open every way, vines and geraniums coming up through the floor and all over the ceiling—birds—fish—fountains— everything that can flutter & splash—& orange garden below.' Dickens had known the Hollands since 1838, and old Lady Holland had written about him: 'we have had the author of Oliver Twist here. He is a young man, very unobtrusive, yet not shy, intelligent in countenance, and alto- gether prepossessing.'

Lord Holland had been born at Holland House, an enormous early Jacobean mansion in Kensington, London, which was mostly destroyed by German incendiary bombs in September 1940. It gave its name to the Holland House Circle, a sparkling assembly of Whig politicians and intellectuals. An anecdote connected with the place might almost have been invented by Dickens. A youth, invited to spend a whole holiday at Holland House, was told that he might have what he liked for dinner. Wise beyond his years, he chose duck and green peas, with an apricot tart to follow. 'My boy,' said Lord Holland, 'if in all the important questions of your life you decide as wisely as you have decided now, you will be a great and good man.'

We are told that during Dickens's stay in Florence he was 'frequently entertained' (Dentler) by Lord and Lady Holland in the Palazzo del Pugliese, though as a matter of fact his name does not appear in their din- ner-book which is now in the British Library. It seems to me likely that he only went once, though we gather from John Forster that he spent a 'very pleasant and very merry day' there. At their receptions and banquets they were accustomed to entertaining not only the English community and English visitors to Florence but also the leading Florentines and visiting

Italians, so it is likely that Dickens met both nationalities at the Hollands' hospitable table.

While he was in Florence Dickens drove up to Fiesole to see the villa formerly occupied by his friend Walter Savage Landor. Some thirty-seven years older than Dickens, Landor admired his young friend and enjoyed his company. Ten years previously, Landor had quarrelled with his wife Julia and had left Italy for England. Dickens was curious and asked his coachman which was the villa in which the Landor family lived. Dickens recalled:

'He was a dull dog and pointed to Boccaccio's. I didn't believe him. He was so deuced ready that I knew he lied. I went up to the convent, which is on a height, and was leaning over a dwarf wall basking in the noble view over a vast range of hill and valley, when a little peasant girl came up and began to point out the localities. *Ecco la villa Landora!* was one of the first half-dozen sentences she spoke. My heart swelled as Landor's would have done when I looked down upon it, nestling among its olive trees and vines... I plucked a leaf of ivy from the convent-garden as I looked; and here it is. For Landor. With my love.'

This is from a letter to John Forster, who wrote biographies of both Landor and Dickens. When Forster was rummaging among Landor's papers, some twenty years later, he came across the very ivy leaf that Dickens had sent, withered but still intact.

While Dickens was in the vicinity of Landor's villa a faintly embarrassing incident occurred that he related to Landor on his return. The coachman suddenly stopped his horses in a narrow lane and presented Dickens to 'La Signora Landora', having inferred that he was about to call at the villa. 'I pulled off my hat... apologised for the coachman's mistake, and drove on. The lady was walking with a rapid and firm step, had bright eyes, a fine fresh colour, and looked animated and agreeable.' When Dickens told Landor about this chance meeting with his estranged wife, Landor 'checked off each clause of the description, with a stately nod of more than ready assent, and replied, with all his tremendous energy concentrated into the sentence: "And the Lord forbid that I should do otherwise than declare that she always WAS agreeable—to every one but *me!*"'

From Florence, evidently from the Oltrarno, Dickens wrote to John Forster:

'There are some p[a]laces here,—oh Heaven how fine! I wish you could see the tower of the Palazzo Vecchio as it lies before me, on the opposite bank of the Arno! But I will tell you more about it, and about all Florence, from my shady arm-chair up among the Peschiere oranges [referring to the Palazzo del Peschiere in Genoa, where the Dickens family was based].'

Rather annoyingly he seems to have forgotten all about this promise, and we hear no more of Florence in Dickens's correspondence.

There are however some more descriptions in *Pictures of Italy.*

'In the midst of the city—in the Piazza of the Grand Duke, adorned with beautiful statues and the Fountain of Neptune—rises the Palazzo Vecchio, with its enormous overhanging battlements, and the Great Tower that watches over the whole town. In its court-yard—worthy of the Castle of Otranto in its ponderous gloom—is a massive staircase that the heaviest wagon and the stoutest team of horses might be driven up.

'Within it is a Great Saloon, faded and tarnished in its stately decorations… but recording yet, in pictures on its walls, the triumphs of the Medici and the wars of the old Florentine people.'

This is Dickens in his travelogue mode, evoking the gloomy courtyard of Palazzo Vecchio with a reference to Horace Walpole's Gothick novel *The Castle of Otranto,* and imagining a wagon and horses being driven up the staircase. But immediately the darker and more sinister Dickens emerges, as his attention is attracted by the nearby prison.

'The prison is hard by, in an adjacent court-yard of the building—a foul and dismal place, where some men are shut up close, in small cells like ovens; and where others look through bars and beg; where some are playing draughts, and some are talking to their friends, who smoke, the while, to purify the air; and some are buying wine and fruit of women-vendors; and all are squalid, dirty, and vile to look at. "They are merry enough, Signore", says the Jailer. "They are all blood-stained here", he adds, indicating, with his hand, three fourths of the whole building.'

And as in E.M. Forster's novel *Room with a View*, in piazza della Signoria there is a sudden irruption of violence and bloodshed. 'Before the hour is out, an old man, eighty years of age, quarrelling over a bargain with a young girl of seventeen, stabs her dead, in the market-place full of bright flowers; and is brought in prisoner, to swell the number.' Dickens's awareness of the pointlessness of the young woman's death is brought out by his mention of the bright flowers.

He was intrigued by the Ponte Vecchio, and by the Vasari Corridor:

'Among the four old bridges that span the river, the Ponte Vecchio—that bridge which is covered with the shops of Jewellers and Goldsmiths—is a most enchanting feature in the scene. The space of one house, in the centre, being left open, the view beyond is shown as in a frame; and that precious glimpse of sky, and water, and rich buildings, shining so quietly among the huddled roofs and gables on the bridge, is exquisite. Above it, the Gallery of the Grand Duke crosses the river. It was built to connect the two Great Palaces by a secret passage; and it takes its jealous course among the streets and houses, with true despotism: going where it lists, and spurning every obstacle away, before it.'

The corridor of some 760 metres was built in only five months in 1565 by Giorgio Vasari for Cosimo I de' Medici: an astonishing feat of engineering.

Dickens was fascinated by the confraternity of the Misericordia, whose members disguise themselves in enveloping black garments with pointy hoods, allowing only the eyes to show. He was especially impressed that the Grand Duke Leopoldo II was a member, and would walk among his subjects in disguise, like Harun al-Rashid in the streets of Bagdad. 'Those who are on duty for the time, are all called together, on a moment's notice, by the tolling of the great bell of the Tower; and it is said that the Grand Duke has been seen, at this sound, to rise from his seat at table, and quietly withdraw to attend the summons.'

He gives a description of the Piazza del Duomo, with the so-called '*Sasso di Dante*', in a little square to the south-east of the Cathedral, which is still to this day a minor tourist attraction:

'In this other large Piazza… are grouped together, the Cathedral with its great Dome, the beautiful Italian Gothic Tower the Campanile, and the Baptistery

"The Effects of the Plague", tableau by Gaetano Giulio Zumbo, ca 1691, Natural History Museum, La Specola

with its wrought bronze doors. And here, a small untrodden square in the pavement, is "the Stone of Dante", where (so runs the story) he was used to bring his stool, and sit in contemplation. I wonder was he ever, in his bitter exile, withheld from cursing the very stones in the streets of Florence the ungrateful, by any kind remembrance of this old musing-place, and its association with gentle thoughts of little Beatrice!'

This is the sort of thing that interests him: he does not refer to a single painting in his descriptions of Florence.

Dickens visited La Specola, in via Romana, where the Natural History Museum had been set up in 1775 by order of the Grand Duke Pietro Leopoldo. Like many others before and since he was fascinated by the wax anatomical models, made over many years by the Opificio di Ceroplastica, for teaching purposes.

Many people find these realistic wax models repulsive and disturbing: the painter Élisabeth Vigée-Lebrun, for instance, saw them in 1792 and felt queasy for several days thereafter. Lady Blessington thought them indecent. Dickens's interest seems to have been not so much scientific as religious: he regarded them above all as a majestic and tragic *memento mori*. 'Few admonitions of our frail mortality', he wrote, 'can be more solemn and more sad, or strike so home upon the heart, as the counterfeits of Youth and Beauty that are lying there, upon their beds, in their last sleep.'

Florence at this time was still a walled city, and Dickens well describes the effect of returning after an expedition into the surrounding countryside:

'Beyond the walls, the whole sweet Valley of the Arno... innumerable spots of interest, all glowing in a landscape of surpassing beauty steeped in the richest light; are spread before us. Returning from so much brightness, how solemn and how grand the streets again, with their great, dark, mournful palaces, and many legends.'

These extracts are from *Pictures of Italy*, published in 1846 by Bradbury & Evans, which was generally poorly reviewed when it came out but which made Dickens a modest profit and is still in print after 175 years.

And this is how Dickens takes his leave of the city: 'Let us look back on Florence while we may, and when its shining Dome is seen no more, go travelling through cheerful Tuscany, with a bright remembrance of it; for Italy will be the fairer for the recollection.'

At the end of his life, still in his late fifties but worn to a frazzling by his punishing schedule of exhausting public readings, especially by his frightening re-enactment of the murder of Nancy by Bill Sykes from *Oliver Twist*, and comforted by his young mistress Ellen Ternan, Dickens said that his memories of Florence remained vivid in his mind like those of no other city.

III

THE LATER NINETEENTH CENTURY

AFTER THE EUROPEAN revolutions of 1848-1849, the return to power of Leopoldo II was supported by the presence of an Austrian garrison, which caused a good deal of popular resentment. In the summer of 1849 Mrs Browning noted that there was a new order that 'all dogs found in the street should be killed straightaway, lest they interfere with the movements of the Austrian horse', and she was so worried about her pet Spaniel that she and Robert left the city for the Bagni di Lucca. Having consulted the conservative powers, Leopoldo revoked the 1848 liberal constitution in 1852. The Austrian garrison of 10,000 men remained in Florence until 1855, while the Grand Duke became increasingly unpopular. In 1859, when Tuscany was on the point of joining the kingdom of northern Italy, Leopoldo peacefully fled Florence very early in the morning on 27 April, never to return, and it was said that at 6.00 a.m. the Revolution 'went to breakfast'. Once the Tuscans became subjects of King Vittorio Emanuele II, their history merged with that of Italy.

The prolific London-born novelist ANTHONY TROLLOPE (1815-1882) used to come to visit his relatives at the Villino Trollope in what is now piazza Indipendenza, and was then known as piazza Maria Antonia in honour of the Grand Duchess, second consort of Leopoldo II. In the Palazzo Pitti a timid tourist once tapped him on the back and asked in a whisper where in Florence was to be found the 'Medical Venus'. (As a matter of fact there are plenty of very medical venuses to be seen in the Specola which is not far away, in via Romana; but what the man wanted was the Medici Venus in the Tribuna at the Uffizi.) While he was here Trollope devised

Anthony Trollope

Isabella Blagden

an eightfold classification for tourists. On his third visit he began to write the novel *Dr Thorne*. The atmosphere of Villino Trollope is evoked in a rather gushing and breathless article by the young American journalist Kate Field in the *Atlantic Monthly* of December 1864: 'Ah, this Villino Trollope is quaintly fascinating, with its marble pillars, its grim men in armor, starting like sentinels from the walls, and its curiosities greeting you at every step. The antiquary revels in its *majolica*, its old Florentine bridal chests and carved furniture, its beautiful terra-cotta of the Virgin and Child by Orgagna [*sic*], its hundred *oggetti* of the Cinque Cento... Here Anthony Trollope is to be found, when he visits Florence; and it is no ordinary pleasure to enjoy simultaneously the philosophic reasoning of Thomas Trollope,—looking half Socrates and half Galileo,—whom Mrs Browning was wont to call "Aristides the Just", and the almost boyish enthusiasm and impulsive argumentation of Anthony Trollope, who is a noble specimen of a thoroughly frank and loyal Englishman. The unity of affection existing between these brothers is as charming as it is rare.'

One member of the Trollope circle was THEODOSIA TROLLOPE (née Garrow, 1816-1865), and she was the subject of a good deal of Anglo-Florentine gossip. It appears that she had an unusually dark-skinned father called Joseph Garrow, the son of an Indian army officer and a high-caste Brahmin woman. Joseph Garrow had married a rich Jewish widow who was twenty-five years his senior and who had some grown-up children. At the remarkable age of fifty-nine, this wife was declared to have given birth to a daughter, Theodosia. One of the grown-up children, called Fanny, took much more interest in little Theodosia than the supposed old mother did, which led the Anglo-Florentine gossips to conclude, no doubt correctly, that Theodosia was the daughter of this Fanny (and not of the fifty-nine-year-old). On the subject of Anglo-Florentine tittle-tattle, there is an interesting note in Charles Richard Weld's book on *Florence, the New Capital of Italy*, published in 1867: 'Everyone concerns himself more or less with his or her neighbour's doings, and acts as a kind of volunteer detective... You must not, then, hope to escape the sharp tongue of gossip if you live in Florence. But be not cast down, for though you may not have a pachyderm mind as regards the talk of your neighbours, you may be quite sure that the gossip will not prove injurious to you.' Theodosia began to publish poetry in 1839 and her work was praised by Walter Savage Landor, who arranged for some of it to be published in Lady Blessington's *Book of Beauty*, though not by Mrs Browning, who thought she lacked 'genius'. She arrived in Florence aged twenty-eight in 1844 and stayed with Fanny Trollope in her house, where she met and married Thomas Adolphus, known as Tom. When her real mother died she left a good deal of money to Theodosia, which is what enabled the Trollopes to move into the Villino on piazza Maria Antonia and to entertain on so lavish a scale. The salon she set up at the Villino as a rival attraction to Casa Guidi was visited by all sorts of artistic and political types. Theodosia had a daughter called Beatrice or Bice, and she continued to publish poetry and prose, writing a lot about the Italian Risorgimento.

ISABELLA BLAGDEN (?1818-1873) was a mysterious Anglo-Indian who settled permanently in Bellosguardo in 1849. She seems to have been born in Calcutta, to an Englishman called Thomas Bracken and to an Indian mother, possibly called Blagden, though not much is known about her earlier life. At one time she shared part of the Villa Brichieri-Colombi with Frances Power Cobbe; at another she was in the Villa Giglione; her favourite was the Villa Castellani (now Mercedes) on the piazza. 'Isa' was an intimate friend of the Brownings and of Theodosia Trollope. Robert Browning once wrote to ask her: 'Whom does one care to tease, that one does not also care to kiss?' George Lewes described her as 'awful' in 1860, but a few years later he went to one of her parties. She wrote a couple of novels and some not very good poems; here is a sample: 'My Florence which so fair doth lie, / A dream of beauty at my feet, / While smiles above the dappled sky, / While glows around the ripening wheat.'

The poet and scholar ARTHUR HUGH CLOUGH (1819-1861) first visited Florence in 1843 with two friends. He is the author of the celebrated lyric 'Say not the struggle naught availeth', which Winston Churchill famously quoted in April 1941, thereby raising the value of Clough's poetical stock. Later in life, after his health broke down in Greece (where he had been translating Homer), he was ordered by a doctor in Paris to go and convalesce in Florence, in order to save his health. He and his wife Blanche (a cousin of Florence Nightingale, with whom Clough was hopelessly in love) arrived in October 1861 and took rooms at the Hotel York in via Cerretani. In that month the Kingdom of Italy was proclaimed. After a week they moved to Casa Fabriani, at piazza Pitti no. 21. Clough was taken for drives to all his favourite places, but was too weak to walk, and held his head painfully on one side. Susan and Joanna Horner, authors of a two-volume guide to Florence and its environs, were extremely kind to Clough. Dr Wilson, Elizabeth Browning's physician, diagnosed his malady as 'Slow Fever.' He moved to piazza Maria Antonia but was clearly on his last legs so his sister Anne was summoned from England. The astonishment of seeing her seems to have finished him off. His funeral at the so-called English cemetery (owned by the Swiss) took place on 15 November, a few months after that of Mrs Browning and a few years before that of Walter Savage Landor. If you go to piazzale Donatello, you can visit the graves of all three poets.

JOHN RUSKIN (1819-1900) was given for his thirteenth birthday a copy of Samuel Rogers' poem *Italy*, and according to him it determined the entire course of his life. Ruskin came to Florence with his parents in 1840, and

John Ruskin

they stayed at the Hotel Schneiderff in lungarno Guicciardini. On 13 November he wrote: 'the Arno [is] a nasty muddy ditch, worse than the Wye at Chepstow, and not much bigger, with reedy mud banks like the Thames at Hounslow.' Twelve days later he left, and noted: 'Glad to get out of stupid Florence.' On 26 April 1841 he wrote: 'Walked in the afternoon. Air warm as an oven, but the town is beyond all doubt a stupid place, and the statues in the great square—even Cellini's Perseus—do not improve upon acquaintance.' He went back four years later, staying at the Grand Hotel Royal in lungarno Acciaiuoli, and began an in-depth study of early Florentine art, making beautiful drawings at Santa Croce, San Marco, Santa Maria Novella, etc.. Ruskin returned often to Florence (e.g. in 1869, 1870, 1872, 1874, 1882, 1884), and usually stayed at the Hotel Arno. His Florentine books are three: *Ariadne Fiorentina* (1873), *Val d'Arno* (1874) and *Mornings in Florence* (1875). As an art critic he is unbearably pompous, prolix and prejudiced. One of his prejudices was that he adored Tintoretto but absolutely loathed Titian. In general Ruskin took a dim view of the Renaissance. Thinking of the Italians made him splutter and foam with rage: he found his hosts to be 'lazy, lousy, scurrilous, cheating, lying, thieving, hypocritical, brutal, blasphemous, obscene, cowardly, earthly, sensual, [and] devilish.' With such thoughts seething in his head, it is hardly surprising that his mind gave way in the end.

QUEEN VICTORIA (1819-1901) visited Florence thrice. She may not seem to be a 'literary' visitor, but the novelist-prime minister Benjamin Disraeli once said to her 'We authors, ma'am…'. in connection with her book *Leaves from the Journal our Life in the Highlands*, published in 1868. Florence had been the favourite city of her beloved German husband Prince Albert,

Tre Vifi. Villa de SS. Palmieri al principio della salita di Fiesole.

Villa Palmieri

who had visited it as a young man and who died in 1861: it was for this reason that she particularly wished to see the city. In 1888 and again in 1893 the Queen-Empress stayed at the Villa Palmieri, as the guest of Lord Crawford, and in 1894 at the Villa Fabbricotti, in via Vittoria Emanuele, on the slopes of Montughi (built thirty years previously), as the guest of Giuseppe Fabbricotti. She came as a private individual ('Madame la Comtesse de Balmoral'). Her Scottish attendants in kilts, and her Indian attendant in a turban, absolutely fascinated the Florentine crowds. To commemorate her visits, the Anglo-Florentine community commissioned a pretty little fountain of reddish marble, adorned with the initials VRI (*Victoria Regina Imperatrix*), in what is now piazza Vittorio Veneto.

The seafaring New York novelist HERMAN MELVILLE (1819-1891) arrived on 24 March 1857, having visited Rome, Leghorn and Pisa. This was six years after the publication of *Moby-Dick*. He had hoped for bright and warm spring weather, but it rained most of the time. 'Florence', he said, 'is a lovely city even on a cold rainy day.' In his journal he wrote: 'Wandered about after leaving gallery Pitti. To the Duomo & Campanile. Came upon

Hermann Melville

George Eliot

them unexpectedly. Amazed by their magnificence. Could not enter. Bought fine mosaics for one Napoleon.' Melville admired the frescoes by Andrea del Sarto at the Santissima Annunziata, and was interested in the wax anatomical models at the Specola, especially the horrific ones by Gaetano Zummo showing the effects of the Plague. He stayed at the Hotel du Nord in Palazzo Bartolini-Salimbeni (piazza Santa Trìnita), and breakfasted each morning at Doney's in via Tornabuoni. It is said that he rarely missed taking afternoon tea, as well, at Doney's. Melville generally dined in the Luna restaurant, on the corner of via della Condotta and vicolo de' Cerchi. He did not think much of the Uffizi, except for Titian's voluptuous *Venus of Urbino*, which he did like a lot.

The Warwickshire novelist GEORGE ELIOT (real name Marian Evans, 1819-1880) came for the first time with her common-law husband George Henry Lewes in May 1860. She thought that unlike Rome, Florence 'looks inviting as one catches sight from the railway of its cupolas and towers and its embosoming hills, the greenest of hills, sprinkled everywhere with white villas.'

The weather was beautiful. They took a comfortable salon and a large bedroom, in the Pension Suisse at the corner of via Tornabuoni and via della Vigna Nuova, just opposite Palazzo Strozzi, paying 10 *paoli* a day (about five shillings, equivalent to £31 in modern money). 'We are at the quietest hotel in Florence', Marian wrote, 'having sought it out for the sake of getting clear of the stream of English and Americans, in which one finds oneself in all the main tracks of travel, so that one seems at last to be in a perpetual noisy picnic, obliged to be civil, though with a strong inclination to be sullen.'

Marian and George spent their mornings sightseeing, carefully recording their impressions in their journals, and in the afternoons they would drive out to the Cascine or the Boboli, to San Miniato or Fiesole. Once they made an excursion to Siena. In her journal Marian described the view from Bellosguardo: 'There is Brunelleschi's mighty dome, and close by it, with its lovely colours not entirely absorbed by distance, Giotto's incomparable campanile, beautiful as a jewel. Further on, to the right, is the majestic tower of the Palazzo Vecchio... then the elegant Badia and the Bargello close by; nearer to us the grand campanile of Santo Spirito, and that of Santa Croce; far away, on the left, the cupola of San Lorenzo, and the tower of Santa Maria Novella.' A few days after her arrival in Florence, Marian made a momentous decision about her next novel, which would be her fourth. George had been reading a guidebook about Gerolamo Savonarola, and he noted: 'it occurred to me that his life and times afford fine material for an historical romance. Polly at once caught at the idea with enthusiasm. It is a subject which will fall in with much of her studies and sympathies; and it will give fresh interest to our stay in Florence.' (Polly was George's pet name for Marian.)

The very next day they went to the convent of San Marco, which had been Savonarola's political headquarters. While Marian contemplated Fra Angelico's great fresco of the *Crucifixion* in the first cloister, George explored the convent for her, as women were not admitted. He made notes on what he found.

In the Magliabecchian Library, at that time housed in the Uffizi, they examined a MS volume by Savonarola, 'written in a minute, shortsighted hand, but very clear.'

In Palazzo Vecchio they visited the Sala del Cinquecento, built in only seven months from July 1495 'under Savonarola's direction', to house the Great Council that was required by his extra-democratic constitution;

and two days later they went to Palazzo Corsini to see the much-repro-
duced painting of the *Execution of Savonarola*, which they seem to have
thought was by Pollaiuolo.

In London the Leweses had been on friendly terms with the prolific
novelist Anthony Trollope. George called at the Villino Trollope, in
piazza Maria Antonia now piazza Indipendenza, hoping to see Anthony's
brother Tom, but he was away. George recorded in his Journal: 'Mrs
Trollope called, bringing with her an awful visitor, a Miss Blagden, who
beset Polly.' Miss Blagden was Isabella Blagden, Browning's 'Dearest Isa.'
She wrote not very good poems, and evidently Marian found her tiresome. Tom Trollope returned to Florence, and Marian and George were
invited to spend the evening at the Villino on 30 May.

Among the other guests were the Irish novelist Charles Lever and
the young American journalist Kate Field. Lever had been very jolly and
amusing as a young man, but now felt rather stale and used-up. He wrote:
'After 38 or so what has life to offer but one universal declension. Let the
crew pump as hard as they like, the leak gains every hour.' Pretty Kate
was not impressed by the visiting couple's physical appearance: 'Miss
Evans, or Mrs Lewes, is a woman whose whole face is of the horse make.
I like Mr Lewes, who is a very ugly man, but very charming in conversation, so that you forget his looks', she wrote to her aunt.

The Trollopes were most welcoming. George noted: 'They showed
us over their house and we descended into the garden, where the fireflies
(the first I have seen) were abundant.' After they left Florence Marian was
relieved to receive good news in Rome about the sales of her latest novel
The Mill on the Floss: 4,600 copies had been shifted within four days of
publication, which was extremely encouraging.

At this point it is worth making a short digression on the life of Fra
Gerolamo Savonarola, around the last six years of which Marian was
to construct her novel. He was born in Ferrara in 1452, the grandson of
a famous physician. As a young man he was ardent and idealistic, and
having apparently been disappointed in love he joined the Dominican
Order in Bologna in 1475. He told his father that he wanted to be a knight
of Christ. Seven years later he was assigned to the convent of San Marco
in Florence. For some years he travelled about as an itinerant preacher,
until at the urging of Pico della Mirandola he was recalled to the city by
Lorenzo de' Medici in 1490. Having overcome the Florentines' resistance

Fra Gerolamo Savonarola preaching

to his harsh Ferrarese accent, he was acclaimed as a great orator and preacher. He had a large hooked nose, a long upper lip, and most beautiful and expressive hands. His prophetic sermons attracted such large congregations that he moved to the Duomo. 'Repent, O Florence, while there is still time. Clothe thyself in the white garments of purification. Wait no longer, for there may be no further time for repentance.' Savonarola terrified people with the horrors of the Divine punishments, and made them weep at the tenderness of the Divine mercy. 'It is not I who preach, but God who speaks through me.' He correctly foretold the deaths of Lorenzo and of Pope Innocent VIII, and his vague prediction of God's scourge coming from across the Alps seemed to be fulfilled when the French king Charles VIII invaded Italy in 1494. Savonarola won the gratitude of the Florentines when he apparently persuaded the French king to withdraw from the city. Soon however he came into conflict with the worldly Spanish pope, Alexander VI Borgia. Although Savonarola held no elected political office, he was the *de facto* dictator of the republic which he had set up after the expulsion of the Medici. Processions of children paraded through the streets, singing his favourite psalm *Ecce quam bonum* and other sacred songs. Wigs, cosmetics, playing cards, dice and lascivious books and paintings were publicly burnt in the so-called

Bonfire of the Vanities. When Savonarola refused to give up control of San Marco, Alexander excommunicated him for disobedience. His star began to wane. The Ordeal by Fire, to which he had been challenged by a Franciscan rival, turned out to be a damp squib, as it was rained off. Public opinion turned against the Friar: he was arrested by the mob, and throughout Holy Week and Easter Week 1498 he was repeatedly tortured. He confessed to being a false prophet, then retracted his confession, then confessed again. Finally he and his two faithful Dominican companions were degraded from the clerical state by the commissioners sent by Alexander, were hanged and burnt in piazza della Signoria, and their ashes were scattered in the Arno. Now, back to Marian and George.

In April 1861 Marian told her publisher Blackwood that she would soon be setting out with 'grave purpose' for Italy, since her two-week stay in Florence in 1860 had not provided her with nearly enough information about the city in the late fifteenth century: she would need a good deal more before feeling able to embark on the huge and amazingly detailed fresco of her forthcoming book. Her plan was to return to Florence and immerse herself in the history and topography of the city, hoping that in some way a narrative would emerge that could be attached to the tragedy of Savonarola. She and George left England on 19 April, the day after his forty-fourth birthday, and a few days after the outbreak of the American Civil War.

Passing through Paris, they visited the tomb of Héloïse and Abélard in the cemetery of Père Lachaise. This was a popular destination for lovers' pilgrimages. In Avignon, Marian was especially keen to see the tomb of the feminist philosopher Harriet Taylor Mill, who had died some three years previously and had been buried by her husband John Stuart Mill. She had been an ardent advocate of women's rights, which is enough to explain Marian's interest in her. In the south of France Marian noted: 'Everywhere a delicious plain covered with bright green corn, sprouting vines, mulberry trees, olives, and here and there meadows sprinkled with buttercups.' (When she writes 'corn', she doesn't mean maize. In traditional English, 'corn' is a generic word for wheat and barley and similar crops.)

After Genoa they reached Pisa, where Marian was feeling a bit under the weather, but the sight of the Campo dei Miracoli 'roused her a little and after some bouillon she was well enough to set forth and enjoy... this marvellous Cathedral, Campo Santo, Baptistery and Campanile.' They took the train to Florence and by seven in the evening were installed at the Albergo della Vittoria, on the river. Later I think they moved to the Hôtel de l'Europe, located inside Palazzo Spini-Feroni, in piazza Santa Trìnita. From one or other of these hotels they sallied forth to study the cloister at Santa Maria Novella, and went to 'feast our eyes on Giotto's tower and the Cathedral', which did not yet have its hideous late-nine-teenth-century façade. 'Dear Florence was lovelier than ever on this second view,' Marian noted, 'and ill health was the only deduction from perfect enjoyment.' Both she and George were afflicted by chills, grippe, headache, sore throat and fever, and in addition she had severe period pains. Nevertheless, they enjoyed walking through the old streets.

They spent five days in the Magliabecchian Library, looking through ancient books and MSS. George noted: 'It is a delightful library to study in, and the books are brought rapidly and without trouble.'

Jackdaw-like, Marian copied into her notebooks all sorts of frag-mentary information about the Florence of Savonarola's day: costume, sumptuary laws, language, dialect, toponyms, family names, descrip-tions of fairs and ceremonies, of bonfires, barbers, jesters, funerals, the making and marketing of woollen cloth. They soon established a daily routine. They got up at seven, breakfasted, then George smoked a cigar. By mid-morning they were out sightseeing in the churches and galler-ies, and visiting the book stalls. They enjoyed 'poking into the curiosi-ties of old Florence', as George wrote to his son. Then they headed for the Magliabecchian Library, where they continued their researches. At two o'clock they lunched, then took a siesta until five or six. After that they drove out or rambled about, sometimes going to the opera. 'We have had glorious sunsets, shedding crimson and golden lights under the dark bridges across the Arno', Marian wrote in a letter. George too made notes and drawings. On Marian's behalf he again visited the parts of the San Marco convent where women were not allowed: 'From [the] refectory a spiral staircase leads to [the] cells—a few paces from the top to the right is the other staircase opposite which is the Annunciation.' The spiral staircase he mentions no longer exists but traces of it can be found on the floor plan, and it is referred to in the novel. He notes that Savonarola's cell is '5 paces long and 4 broad', so presumably he paced it out for her.

Although Florence was at this time home to several major writers such as Walter Savage Landor and Robert and Elizabeth Browning, the Leweses did not see many people during their five weeks in the city. We should always remember that they were not considered a respectable couple, being unmarried. Only progressive or Bohemian types were likely to meet them socially. An English painter called Jane Benham Hay, whom they had met the previous year at the Villino Trollope, came to call on them at their hotel. She had left her English husband and was living in Florence with an Italian painter, Francesco Altamura. In 1867 she had a success with her painting of *The Bonfire of the Vanities*.

Tom Trollope was out of town, but they saw his wife Theodosia and his ten-year-old daughter Bice on several occasions. As usual there were interesting people at the Villino, and both Italians and English sat about in the cool loggia, drinking lemonade and smoking.

One of the company was Colonel John Whitehead Peard, known as 'Garibaldi's Englishman', who had a 'fine massive energetic head' and a 'huge iron-grey beard.' He was evidently a reading man, for I found his signature in the members' book of the Gabinetto Vieusseux lending library. The Leweses were very impressed by Colonel Peard, but I am sorry to report that one of his underlings described him as 'a bloodthirsty man who, unable to gratify his penchant for murders in his own country, comes out here and gloats over his victims.'

Another friend of the Trollopes, Signor Tibaldi, gave them tickets for a ceremony in memory of the Tuscan heroes of 1848, held in the Basilica of Santa Croce on 29 May. The church was hung with drapery, and all the side altars were ablaze with lights. In the centre stood a huge catafalque with a crowned angel standing before it. The aisles were lined with troops, and a military band struck up the dead march, which they found extremely moving. After the Mass an impassioned sermon was preached by a small blind priest, Padre Angelico, whose delivery was recalled by Marian when she came to describe Savonarola preaching in the Duomo.

On Tom Trollope's return he persuaded them to undertake an expedition to Camaldoli and La Verna, which they did, going part of the way by pony. They enjoyed the monasteries, and George's Journal is full of monastic routine. Tom Trollope, by the bye, was engaged on writing a four-volume *History of Florence*, and he turned out to be an excellent source of historical information about the city.

Before they left Florence in early June they called at the Villino to say farewell, and there they heard the sad news of the death of Cavour. This same sad news pretty much finished off Elizabeth Browning, who died some three weeks later at Casa Guidi.

Back in England, Marian embarked on a massive reading programme, to fill in the gaps of her knowledge of late-fifteenth-century Florence. She read widely and deeply in both the primary and the secondary sources. She had tremendous difficulties in writing her novel as she suffered acutely from 'writer's block', a phenomenon first described in 1947 by the Austrian psychotherapist Edmund Bergler. (Bergler, incidentally, blamed oral masochism, bottle-feeding and an unstable private love life for the difficulties authors face in carrying out their projects.) *Romola* was published in fourteen monthly instalments in *The Cornhill Magazine*, between July 1862 and August 1863. It has always been the least read of her books, though she wrote of it: 'There is no book of mine about which I more thoroughly feel that I swear by every sentence as having been written with my best blood' and 'I began it a young woman—I finished it an old woman'. Whereas 6,000 copies of *The Mill on the Floss* were sold within two months of publication, it took a year to sell the 1,700 copies of *Romola* and it was then remaindered. Ordinary readers found it a disappointment—it was accused of 'instructive antiquarianism'—but the London intelligentsia pressed the novel to its bosom. Robert Browning, who first called on the Leweses in December 1862, told Marian that *Romola* was 'the noblest and most heroic prose poem' he had ever read. Anthony Trollope admired the heroine's character and was sure the novel would outlive its author. Gladstone effusively praised the book at a dinner party. Henry James called it 'the most important of George Eliot's works'. It was admired by Mazzini, Tennyson, Monkton Milnes, Bulwer Lytton, Millais and F.D. Maurice, among many others. A critic in the *Westminster Review* wrote: 'It cannot be denied that *Romola* is less popular than its predecessors, but we do not hesitate to say that it is its author's greatest work.' The *Spectator* called it 'one of the greatest works of modern fiction.'

In 1869 Marian stayed for five days at the Villa Trollope, Ricorboli, the suburban house that Thomas Adolphus had bought from the Altoviti after he sold the one in piazza Maria Antonia (by then renamed piazza Indipendenza). She was ill in bed for most of the time. Despite his sciatica George went to a party given by Isa Blagden, having evidently decided she was not so 'awful' after all. On their last day in Florence Marian was strong

Monument to Florence Nightingale in Sta Croce   *Florence Nightingale*

enough to accompany George to see Professor Schiff demonstrate a device that measured the speed of thought. Moritz Schiff had been appointed professor of physiology at the University of Florence in 1862. His experiments on cats and dogs at La Specola, though scientifically useful, incurred the wrath of the anti-vivisectionist Frances Power Cobbe.

The most eminent English person to be born in Florence was undoubtedly FLORENCE NIGHTINGALE (1820-1910). Her birth took place on 14 May at the Villa la Colombaia, not far from the Porta Romana, which her rich parents had rented. They already had another daughter, Frances Parthenope, who had been born in Naples in 1819: Parthenope ('she who appears to be a virgin') is the Greek name for Naples. Little Florence was christened on 4 July 1820 at the villa, and when she was aged one the family left Italy. I am not aware that she ever returned to the city of her birth. There is a monument to the foundress of modern nursing in the cloister of the basilica of Santa Croce, carved in white Carrara marble and grey pietra serena by Francis William Sargant in 1913. Villa la Colombaia can be found in via Santa Maria a Marignolle, n. 2; it is now a convent of sisters, the Adorers of the Most Precious Blood of Christ.

FRANCES POWER COBBE (1822-1904) lived on and off in Florence from 1857 onwards, usually in Bellosguardo. At one time she was staying with Isa Blagden in the Villa Brichieri-Colombi, which looks out over Florence and over Scandicci; at another time she had rooms in the Villa Niccolini. She was a friend of the statesman Massimo d'Azeglio and of the sculptor Pasquale Romanelli, also of Walter Savage Landor, the Brownings and the Trollopes. She was a great reformer and one of her sayings was 'Power is my middle name', which was also true. She collected signatures against cruel experiments such as those of Moritz Schiff. Kate Field thought her 'the embodiment of genial philanthropy', and told the following anecdote: 'Upon [her] expostulating one day with a coachman who was beating his poor straw-fed horse most unmercifully, the man replied, with a look of wonderment, *"Ma, che vuole, Signora? non è cristiano!"* (But what would you have, Signora? he is not a Christian!). Not belonging to the Church, and having no soul to save, why should a horse be spared the whip? The reasoning is not logical to our way of thinking, yet it is Italian, and was delivered in good faith. It will require many Miss Cobbes to lead the Italians out of their Egypt of ignorance.'

In the mid-1860s, Crowe and Cavalcaselle published their *A New History of Painting in Italy*. Of the *Venus of Urbino*, they wrote: 'Not after the model of a Phryne [the Athenian courtesan who posed for Apelles], nor yet with the thought of realising anything more sublime than woman in her fairest aspect, did Titian conceive this picture. Nature as he presents it here is young and lovely, not transfigured into ineffable noblesse, but conscious and triumphant, without loss of modesty'.

The poet and educationalist MATTHEW ARNOLD (1822-1888) visited Florence many times in his capacity as school inspector (for purposes of comparison), always staying at the Hotel de Florence in borgo Ognissanti, later the Pensione Novella. In May 1865, when he came for an interview with the Minister of Public Instruction, Matthew wrote to his wife Frances Lucy: 'It was for this country that I was predestined, for I found everything just as I expected.' He described the approach to the city: 'The cypresses on every height, round every villa or convent, are the effect that pleases me most. But the whole country is a pell-mell of olive, vine, mulberry, fig,

Matthew Arnold

Alfred Austin

maize, and wheat all the way to Florence.' He preferred the Duomo to any other church he had seen in Christendom: in a letter to his sister he wrote: 'I am sorry you were tormented by the mosquitoes at Florence; they are enough to spoil anything; but Florence is the most enchanting place I know in the world... It took me by surprise when I arrived one beautiful morning in May. The Cathedral outside (not inside) is to my feeling the most beautiful church in the world, and it always looks to me like a hen gathering its chickens under its wings, it stands in such a soft, lovely way, with Florence round it. Then never did pictures give me the pleasure that the pictures in those two great galleries [Uffizi and Pitti] did. Andrea del Sarto and Fra Bartolomeo, two artists who touch me particularly, are not to be known without going to Florence. And San Miniato, and the [view of the] Carrara mountains, and Fiesole! But I must not go on about Florence.' Late in 1887 he wrote to an American friend in Florence that he was thinking of moving there: 'It is the most beautiful place I know.' However, Matthew found it hard to leave his lovely cottage and garden in Cobham, and the following spring was his last.

The walrus-moustached poetaster ALFRED AUSTIN (1835-1913) stayed for two weeks in 1862. He said that although Florence was not large, all the greatness in painting, sculpture, literature, architecture and history was to be found here. He was back in the autumn of 1864, and stayed until the following spring. At first he lived in two furnished rooms at no. 14 lungarno Acciaiuoli (building destroyed by bombing), then he took a few rooms in the Villa Bigazzi at Bellosguardo. He was elected a member of the Circolo dell'Unione, where he took his meals. (The Circolo is a convincing imitation of a London club, decorated with sporting prints and hunting trophies, though the cooking is most superior.) After Theodosia Trollope died on 17 April, Austin went to stay with Tom Trollope in the piazza dell'Indipendenza. In 1866 he came with his new bride Hester Jane Homan-Mulock, to spend the summer with Trollope in his new villa at Ricorboli. Apparently he had seen Hester's photograph in an album and on asking who she was received the reply: 'The girl you ought to marry, if you can.' They became engaged at their second meeting, and married on 14 November 1865. In the autumn of 1869 they stayed with the Marquis de Boissy at Villa Nito at Settimello near Calenzano. The marquis was inordinately proud of the fact that his wife Teresa, the former Contessa Guiccioli, had been Byron's last mistress, and introduced her to people as such. In the spring of 1887 Austin stayed at Villa Caprini in Fiesole, as the guest of Lady Paget and her daughter Lady Windsor. In 1896 the untalented Austin succeeded Tennyson as Poet Laureate, no doubt because of his political support for the Conservative Lord Salisbury, and the next year he took a year's lease on the Villa I Cedri. He and his wife returned to Florence in the spring of 1901 and stayed at the Villa Favorita, in a lovely position between via Senese and via del Podestà. In the summer he rented Villa Le Fontanelle, near Careggi; it pleased him to think that this is where Marsilio Ficino had been living when he translated Plato into Latin, and where he wrote his eulogy to Dante.

The American humourist MARK TWAIN (real name Samuel Clemens, 1835-1910) came four times to Florence, twice as a visitor and twice as a resident. He stopped here in 1867 for a short time during a tour of Europe, which resulted in his satirical *Innocents Abroad* (1869): 'It is popular to admire the Arno. It is a great historical creek with four feet in the channel and some

Mark Twain

Oscar Browning

scows [flat-bottomed boats] floating around. It would be a very plausible river if they could pump some water into it. They all call it a river, and they honestly think it *is* a river do these dark and bloody Florentines. They even help out the delusion by building bridges over it. I do not see why they are too good to wade.' In 1878 he again visited Florence during a walking tour of Europe and was most impressed by Titian's painting of *Moses*, which he thought was worth the whole journey to see this one picture. He had it copied, and also engraved. There is however no such picture: Titian did not paint a *Moses*, though Paul Delaroche did. In pretending that Delaroche's modern painting was by the sixteenth-century master, Mark Twain may have been trying to ridicule Titian, whom he (like Ruskin) intensely disliked; he regarded the lovely *Venus of Urbino* in the Uffizi as the 'foulest, the vilest, the obscenest picture that the world possesses.' But he seems to have been genuinely fond of the city: 'To see the sun sink down, drowned on his pink and purple and golden floods, and overwhelm Florence with tides of color that make all the sharp lines dim and faint and turn the solid city to a city of dreams, is a sight to stir the coldest nature, and make a sympathetic one drunk with ecstasy', he wrote. In September 1892 he settled with his wife Olivia and their children into the Villa Viviani (now Belvedere) at Settignano. There he wrote *Pudd'nhead Wilson*, a tale of two very differently situated boys who are switched in infancy. They left the following autumn, returning in November 1903 to live at the Villa di Quarto where Twain wrote his novel *Tom Sawyer Abroad*. His invalid wife found the Florentine climate suited her, and Twain decided to buy a large villa in 1904, but Olivia's death from heart failure put paid to this scheme.

LEADER SCOTT (real name Lucy Baxter, née Barnes, 1837-1902) settled in Florence after her marriage to Thomas Baxter. His family had long resided in Tuscany, and the couple lived at his Villa Bianca near Fiesole. She befriended her neighbour John Temple Leader, the extremely rich former MP who owned the castle of Vincigliata, to the east of Fiesole, and who had had to leave England in a hurry, apparently after a homosexual scandal. Her penname 'Leader Scott' was a tribute to Temple Leader and to Sir Walter Scott, both of whom she admired; or else it might have been a combination of the maiden names of her two grandmothers, Isabel Leader and Grace Scott. It had been chosen for her by her learned father, the Dorset poet William Barnes. She wrote a great many books with titles like *A Nook in the Apennines* (1879), *Tuscan Studies and Sketches* (1887), *Echoes of Old Florence* (1894), as well as a great deal of art history. In December 1882 she was made an honorary member of the Accademia del Disegno. She made friends with the Dorset novelist Thomas Hardy and his first wife Emma, who stayed at the Villino Trollope after it had become an hotel, in the spring of 1887. In May that year the charmless modern façade of Santa Maria del Fiore, designed by Emilio De Fabris, was inaugurated by King Umberto and Queen Margherita. The queen threw an electric switch that caused the canvas coverings to fall off the new façade. Lucy Baxter died in via San Leonardo, at no. 60.

The Cambridge educationalist and misogynist OSCAR BROWNING (1837-1923) said that every lover of Italy has his favourite city, and added: 'I confess myself a Florentine without reserve... Florence was, and always will be, the intellectual capital of Italy. No town in Italy will present that country with genius in literature and art comparable to the mighty dead whose monuments fill the nave of Santa Croce.' He came the first time with his friend Francis Warre-Cornish in the spring of 1861, and stayed at the Hotel d'Italia in what is now piazza Ognissanti, pretending to himself that he was in the Palazzo Murat in Positano, home of Queen Carolina of Naples. This was because some of her furniture was in the hotel. He always stayed there until his last visit in 1884. In the winter of 1862-1863 he enjoyed a lot of socialising in parallel with his literary and historical studies, and he assiduously frequented the Villino Trollope, despite its company of females. He didn't think much of the changes made to Florence when it was the capital of Italy: 'Very few of the alterations in Florence have been improvements; being on a larger scale, they disturb the proportion on which the city was built. The large building on the south side of the Piazza della Signoria dwarfs the excellent Loggia de' Lanzi and impairs the dignity of the Palazzo Vecchio itself, while the Viale de' Colli throws the fortified Monastery of San Miniato into insignificance.' In the spring of 1871 he was at the Villa Mozzi in Fiesole, then called Villa Spence. Browning especially enjoyed the winter of 1874-1875, which he called his 'intellectual banquet'. He met Gino Capponi, General La Marmora and many other Florentine men. Browning's misogyny was asserted by Virginia Woolf, who saw him as a great enemy of female education. In the spring and summer of 1884, his final visit, he stayed at the Hotel d'Europe in the Palazzo Spini-Feroni, with his close friend Francis Money-Coutts, 5th Baron Latymer. Browning published the results of his Florentine studies in *Dante: his Life and Writings* (1891), *Guelfs and Ghibellines* (1893) and *The Age of the Condottieri* (1895).

The poet and dramatist ALGERNON CHARLES SWINBURNE (1837-1909) travelled in February 1864 to Paris in company with his friend Lord Houghton, previously known as Richard Monckton Milnes. After a few days he left Houghton in Paris and pressed on to Italy, armed with Houghton's letter of introduction, specifically in order to pay homage to the great Walter Savage Landor in Florence. He stayed at the Albergo Gran Bretagna. The twenty-six-year-old Swinburne had a shock of red hair, but otherwise had a great deal in common with Landor, or so he thought. Both were Hellenists, both were atheists and republicans, both idolised the second-generation Romantic poet Percy Bysshe Shelley. Swinburne was entranced by the notion of receiving the poetic torch from one who had been born in 1775 and might well have known Shelley. (In fact Landor never did meet Shelley, because he avoided him on account of his reputation for immorality, to his later regret.) Swinburne's first meeting with Landor was not a success. The young poet wrote to Lord Houghton on 31 March 1864: 'With much labour I hunted out the most ancient of demigods at 93 Via della Chiesa, but (although knock-down blows were not, as you anticipated, his mode of salutation) I found him, owing I suspect to the violent weather, too much weakened and confused to realise the fact of the introduction without distress. In effect, he seemed so feeble and incompatible that I came away in a grievous state of disappointment and depression myself, fearing that I was really too late'.

Apparently he had thrown himself at Landor's feet and covered his hands with kisses, and the irascible old man had been more bewildered than pleased. Swinburne's letter goes on: 'I wrote him a line of apology and explanation, saying why and how I had made up my mind to call upon him after you had furnished me with an introduction... To which missive of mine came a note of invitation which I answered by setting off again for his lodgings. After losing myself for an hour in Borgo S. Frediano I found it at last, and found him as alert, brilliant and delicious as I suppose others may have found him twenty years since.' (It may seem stupid of Swinburne to have got lost for an hour in borgo San Frediano, especially as he had already been once to the house, but my guess is that people were not able to direct him very well as the name of the street had only the previous year been changed from via Nunziatina to via della Chiesa.) Swinburne made various protestations of devotion, and begged Landor to accept the dedication of his forthcoming book of poetry, 'Atalanta in Calydon'. Having graciously accepted, Landor insisted on giving Swinburne a painting which he said was by Correggio—'a masterpiece that was intercepted on its way back to its Florentine home from the Louvre, whither it had been taken by Napoleon Bonaparte'—but which unfortunately turned out to be a fake, like so many of Landor's pictures. Of Titian's *Venus of Urbino*, Swinburne pointed out to Lord Houghton that she has 'four lazy fingers buried dans les fleurs de son jardin'.

A few days after Swinburne's second visit, and while he was contemplating a third, Landor sent him a note (addressed simply to 'Swinburne, Esq'.): 'My dear friend, So totally am I exhausted that I can hardly hold my pen, to express my vexation that I shall be unable ever to converse

Algernon Charles Swinburne   *Kate Field*

with you again. Eyes and intellect fail me—I can only say that I was much gratified by your visit, which must be the last, and I remain ever Your obliged W. Landor.'

If Swinburne was disappointed by this second rebuff, he never said so: I suspect that he had already got what he wanted.

The journalist KATE FIELD (1838-1896) arrived aged twenty-one in the spring of 1859 from St Louis Missouri and stayed in via de' Serragli. She had been a precocious child and was already a well-established journalist. She studied *bel canto* with maestro Rononi, and later moved to a house just opposite the Villino Trollope in piazza Maria Antonia. Kate wrote gushing articles about Florence in American magazines. She was friends with Isa Blagden, the Brownings and the Trollopes; she took Latin lessons with the aged Landor, who delighted in her company; they had been introduced to one another by Anthony Trollope. Kate told her aunt that Marian Evans looked like a horse, and that George Lewes was 'a very ugly man'. After Elizabeth Browning's death and the departure of Isa and Pen, 'Florence became so sad a place' for her that she decamped to the United States.

Villa Stibbert

FREDERICK STIBBERT (1838-1906) was not a visitor because he was born in Florence, of an English father and an Italian mother. An interesting letter written in 1846 by his father Colonel Thomas Stibbert (whose mistress Giulia had several children by him before he married her) explains his choice of where to live: 'The motive that has induced me to fix my residence in Florence is the mildness of the climate, the protection afforded to all foreigners, and the liberty of living unfettered by any restraint or odious civil obligations. Hitherto I have not made the purchase of a house but have taken up my quarters in one of the most select streets of Florence [via del Cocomero, now via Ricasoli]; and which I have consequently furnished as becomes my rank in Society and the respect I owe to my lady and the comforts of my little family'. Frederick was educated at Harrow and Cambridge, fought as a soldier for Garibaldi in 1866 and was given a silver medal, but the main point about him is that he was extremely rich and was able to indulge his eccentric collecting enthusiasms without financial restraint. His monument is the somewhat peculiar Villa Stibbert on the hill of Montughi, stuffed with pictures, furniture, tapestries, arms and armour, Japanese costumes, etc. It has a famous 'cavalcade' of mounted

Ouida

Walter Pater

knights in armour, some of which may even be genuine. Like all very rich collectors he was often taken for a ride by the shady dealers he patronised. In 1861, the year the Kingdom of Italy was proclaimed, Frederick joined the Masonic Lodge known as 'Concordia'. Queen Victoria signed his visitors' book in 1894. Stibbert never married, and his property was eventually inherited by the city of Florence. His tomb, the size of a small house, is in the Allori cemetery in via Senese.

OUIDA (real name Maria Louise Ramé, though she preferred the more aristocratic-sounding Louise de la Ramé, 1839-1908) arrived in Florence with her mother in 1871, and stayed for twenty-three years. Max Beerbohm called her 'that unique, flamboyant lady, one of the miracles of modern literature', and indeed in her time she was a best-selling novelist, though her reputation has now collapsed. (Except in Japan, where she is still popular, thanks to the anime cartoons of her stories.) According to the Irish diarist William Allingham, Ouida had a 'voice like a carving knife' and a 'clever, sinister face'. She liked living in hotels and first of all moved into the Hôtel d'Italie, in piazza Ognissanti (now the Excelsior), and plunged into the exciting social whirl. Before long she fell in love with a handsome and charming nobleman, the Marchese della Stufa, who had become the *cavaliere servente* of Janet Ross (née Duff-Gordon). Mrs Ross lived with her banker husband in the Marchese's Villa Castagnolo at Lastra a Signa. The Marchese della Stufa—according to the novelist Francis King, who had it from Bernard Berenson in 1948—was secretly homosexual, which is why he rather liked to encourage his two admirers, Ouida and Janet Ross, so that they would cover his tracks. His name was Lotteringo Lotteringhi della Stufa and he was known as Lotto. Mrs Ross was outraged that a vulgar upstart of a best-selling novelist should be messing with her beloved *cavaliere servente*, while Ouida, who had convinced herself that Lotto was longing to marry her, and who was now renting the Villa Farinola in Scandicci, promptly wrote a frothy three-volume novel, *Friendship* (1878), all about a ghastly woman called Lady Joan Challoner, very obviously based on Janet Ross, who blackmails an unfortunate young man into staying with her against his will. All hell broke loose, or at any rate there was a storm in the teacup of Anglo-Florentine society, which promptly split into two camps, just like the Guelfs and Ghibellines. Ouida made an unseemly public appeal to the Marchese, as he was emerging from his club; there was talk of a libel action; when the two ladies' carriages unfortunately got stuck next to each other in via Tornabuoni, Janet Ross laid into her rival with a whip. Years afterwards, her niece Lina Waterfield reported that Mrs Ross kept an unbound copy of the offending novel in her downstairs lavatory, for the use of her guests. Poor Ouida went into a decline, 'half-demented over her disappointed hopes', and became more extravagant than ever. She quarrelled with her landlord, and was thrown out by his peasants armed with pitchforks, so she moved into a thirty-room apartment in the Palazzo Magnani Feroni in via de' Serragli. A succession of progressively less grand rented apartments followed—Villa della Corona in Bellosguardo, where Walburga Lady Paget visited her, and Villa La Camorra—until she finally decamped to Lucca and died in poverty in Viareggio in 1908 (as I mentioned earlier she is buried at the Bagni di Lucca).

Her final years were sweetened by a grant from the Royal Literary Fund, which still does good work in this sort of way.

At the time of Oscar Wilde's trials for 'gross indecency', Ouida had written sensibly: 'It may be immoral of me but I do not think the law should meddle with these offences. The publicity caused does much more harm than the offence itself.'

The Oxford aesthete WALTER PATER (1839-1894) first came to Florence in 1865, having just visited Ravenna where he studied the early Christian mosaics. He saw what he considered to be 'the one great picture' Leonardo had left in Florence, the *Head of the Medusa* in the Uffizi, though it is now attributed to Caravaggio. Pater wrote gorgeous and finely cadenced prose. His most celebrated remark is: 'To burn always with this hard, gem-like flame, to maintain this ecstasy, is success in life.' He returned many times to Florence between 1870 and 1890, sometimes spending long periods gathering material for such books as *Sandro Botticelli* (1870), *The Poetry of Michelangelo* (1873) and *Luca della Robbia* (1897)

The pessimistic Dorset novelist THOMAS HARDY (1840-1928) came in the spring of 1887 with his first wife Emma, after visiting Turin, Genoa and Pisa. He had already published *Far from the Madding Crowd* (1874) and *The Mayor of Casterbridge* (1886). They stayed at the Pensione Trollope, as it was called, in the former Trollope residence on piazza Indipendenza. Lucy Baxter, daughter of Hardy's Dorset neighbour the Revd William Barnes, came to see them. Hardy's method of sightseeing was extremely slow and thorough. He liked walking to piazza Signoria and sitting for hours under the Loggia de' Lanzi. Also, he liked wandering out into the countryside. He would amble along via Senese (now cluttered up with petrol stations) as far as the Certosa di Galluzzo, where he would prowl about the empty spaces. With Lucy Baxter the Hardys went several times to Fiesole and examined the Roman theatre: his sonnet on Fiesole is entitled 'In the old theatre'. Hardy enjoyed the events of Holy Week, especially the '*Scoppio del Carro*', with its flower-decorated oxen, its fireworks, its rejoicing crowds, and its zooming artificial dove.

The well-connected writer and historian JANET ROSS (née Duff-Gordon, 1842-1927) came to Florence with her banker husband Henry in the late 1860s. They had been living in Egypt, until Henry's banking career collapsed in the Egyptian financial crisis of 1867 and they had to find somewhere not too expensive to live. At first they rented apartments, initially on the lungarno Acciaiuoli and then on the lungarno Torrigiani, until they decided to rent the Villa Castagnolo at Lastra a Signa to the west of

Janet Ross

Thomas Hardy

Florence, from its owner the Marchese della Stufa. (It was while she was living at the Villa Castagnolo that Mrs Ross had her famous falling-out with the novelist Ouida, q.v..) Janet Ross wrote all sorts of books such as *Italian Sketches* (1887), *The Land of Manfred* (1889), *Leaves from our Tuscan Kitchen, Or, How to Cook Vegetables* (1900), *Old Florence and Modern Tuscany* (1904), *Florentine Palaces and their Stories* (1905). In 1888 the Rosses bought the Villa di Poggio Gherardo at Settignano to the east of Florence. She managed its estate like an 'autocratic empress', selling its produce, including a famous vermouth, and dealing in art. She discovered, and sold for a large profit, Luca Signorelli's *School of Pan*. As a child she had known Thackeray, Dickens, Carlyle and Tennyson; having been very glamorous and dashing as a young woman (in 1863 she travelled by camel to Tell El Kabir, dressed in Bedouin robes and with a hawk on her wrist), Janet gradually evolved into the *grande dame* recalled by Kenneth Clark in his memoirs, dressing always in white—wool in the day, silk in the evening—and terrifying her visitors. Her niece and ward was Lina Duff-Gordon, whom she adopted in 1890 and who later married the painter Aubrey Waterfield. When the young Virginia Woolf visited Mrs Ross, she noted that Lina had 'beautiful eyes'.

The New York novelist HENRY JAMES (1843-1916) visited Florence for the first time in October 1869. Leon Edel, author of the standard five-volume biography, writes that 'from the first it caught his fancy as no other city in Italy: the Tuscan palaces with their pure symmetry had for him the nobility of Greek architecture.' Nine years previously Tuscany had been united to the new kingdom of Italy, and Florence was now its capital. These were exciting times, for James was in Italy during the final months of the Risorgimento. And the beauty of the city delighted him. 'Everything about Florence', he told his father, 'seems to be coloured with a mild violet, like diluted wine.'

In Florence he studied the art in the Uffizi and Pitti galleries, in the Bargello and the Accademia, and he explored the city on foot, including its expanding suburbs. He had casual encounters with Americans, some of whom he seems to have known already: 'Yesterday I met in the Uffizi Miss Anna Vernon of Newport and her friend Mrs Carter, with whom I had some discourse; and on the same morning I fell in with a somewhat seedy and sickly American, who seemed to be doing the gallery with an awful minuteness.' His brother William asked him in a letter how the Americans compared with the English, and he replied most emphatically: 'The English I have met not only kill, but bury in unfathomable depths, the Americans I have met.' This notorious letter, in which he rails at the vulgarity of his fellow countrymen ('vulgar, vulgar, vulgar'), is best seen as an expression of his exaggerated philo-Europeanism.

After visiting the Sagrestia Nuova at San Lorenzo, he wrote to his sister Alice with genuine eloquence about Michelangelo's statues: 'As they sit brooding in their dim-lighted chapel, exhaling silence and thought, they form, I imagine, the most impressive work of art in the world. The warrior with the cavernous visage is absolutely terrible: he seems to shed an amount of inarticulate sorrow sufficient to infest the Universe.'

On 26 October he took a walk from the Porta Romana along via Senese, passing a couple of rows of tenements before reaching open country. At Galluzzo he was enchanted to discover a Carthusian monastery resembling a medieval fortress and 'lifting against the sky, around the bell tower of its gorgeous chapel, a kind of coronet of clustered cells'. Making his way past a gang of crippled beggars who brandished their stumps at him, he gained admittance and was shown by the monks all

Henry James

over the Certosa, which he very much liked. On the 30th he left Florence for Rome.

He was back in Cambridge Massachusetts in 1870, and his first novel, *Watch and Ward*, was published in Boston. In later years it embarrassed him and he disowned it, claiming that his real first novel was *Roderick Hudson*. For three years from 1872 he travelled with his sister Alice and their aunt in France and Italy, mostly in Paris and Rome.

In Florence he met up with his brother William, the future author of *Varieties of Religious Experience*, and they stayed together at the Hôtel de Ville in what is now piazza Ognissanti. Henry wrote to their father about William: 'He is very much charmed with Florence and spends a great deal of time going about the streets and to the galleries.' Henry was trying to work on his novel *Roderick Hudson*, which is set in Rome, so he had to send his brother away in the mornings: only when his morning's work was done would he agree to lunch with William and to explore with him the artistic treasures of the city.

William's favourite painting in the whole of Florence was the *Baptism of Christ* by Paolo Veronese, above a doorway in the Palatine Gallery of Palazzo Pitti—a surprising choice, and far from easy to see. In May 1874 Henry attended 'for information's sake' a 'very brilliant ball' given by the Jockey Club at their Casino in the Cascine: there was 'a concentration of the elite of Florentine society', with 'more tiaras of diamonds, ropes of pearl and acres of *point de Venise* [lace]' than he could shake a stick at.

At this time he was living in piazza Santa Maria Novella, where he had taken an apartment on the second floor of a house on the corner with via della Scala. It had a large, high-ceilinged, charmingly shabby sitting room, and two bedrooms, so he could have his sister to stay. In the spring and early summer that year he came really to love Florence, and he told his friends the Howellses that it seemed to him like a familiar literary masterpiece that one reads and re-reads with constant pleasure. He discovered a lovely French restaurant in via Rondinelli, which displayed lobsters and truffles in its window, and he dined there delightedly with William. Henry returned to New York and from 1874 to 1875 wrote literary journalism for the *Nation* and published three books: *Transatlantic Sketches*, *A Passionate Pilgrim* and the novel *Roderick Hudson*.

Henry James's *Italian Hours* (1909) has a chapter called 'Italy revisited', written in 1877: it contains a vivid description of the houses backing onto the Arno in Florence, seen from his hotel room. 'There was an absurd orange-coloured paper on the walls; the Arno, of a hue not altogether different, flowed beneath; and on the other side of it rose a row of sallow houses, of extreme antiquity, crumbling and mouldering, bulging and protruding over the stream. All this brightness and yellowness was a perpetual delight; it was part of that indefinably charming colour which Florence always seems to wear as you look up and down at it from the river, and from the bridges and quays. This is a kind of grave radiance—a harmony of high tints—which I scarce know how to describe. There are yellow walls and green blinds and red roofs, there are intervals of brilliant brown and natural-looking blue; but the picture is not spotty nor gaudy, thanks to the distribution of the colours in large and comfortable masses, and to the washing-over of the scene by some happy softness of sunshine. The river-front of Florence is in short a delightful composition.' In 1878 James's story 'Daisy Miller' established his fame on both sides of the Atlantic.

He arrived in Florence on 28 March 1880, checked into the Grand Hôtel de l'Arno on lungarno Acciaiuoli, and lost no time in calling on his friends Francis and Lizzie Boott, father and daughter, in Bellosguardo. Two days later he wrote to Henry James Sr: 'The Bootts are the same old Bootts as ever—gentle and affectionate and appreciative.' Francis Boott had been born in Boston in 1813. His rich family owned textile mills, and he went to Harvard University. In 1844 he married Elizabeth Lynam, also from Boston, and their daughter Lizzie was born two years later. A year after that, Boott's wife Elizabeth died. He took his little daughter to Italy where he began to compose music, mostly art songs and sacred works. In 1858 he rented an apartment in the Villa Castellani at Bellosguardo. Clever Lizzie wrote poems and a novel, and began to study painting. They returned to Boston in 1865, where Henry James first met them. Eleven years later Francis and Lizzie settled permanently in Europe, first in France and then in Italy.

In the late 1870s Lizzie Boott fell in love with the penniless, Bohemian and more or less uneducated American artist Frank Duveneck. It is easy to imagine what her patrician and super-protective father felt about this possible match: not only was the working-class Duveneck a Roman Catholic, but he had a reputation for carousing in German beer halls. Born in Kentucky and raised in Cincinnati, the good-natured Duveneck had studied art at the Munich Academy and had founded his own art school in Bavaria. His rowdy American students were known as 'the Duveneck boys'. Lizzie wrote about him to a Boston friend: 'He is a remarkable looking young man. He has a fine head and a keen eye, and the perceptions strongly developed.' She persuaded Duveneck to leave Munich and come to Florence, bringing all his students with him. Since none of them spoke Italian, Lizzie arranged studio space and accommodation for them in Florence. They seem to have made a great impact on the city. James watched benevolently over Lizzie's love for Duveneck. Unlike his friend Francis, he thought the marriage rather a good idea, and in November 1879 he wrote to his brother William: 'The natural and logical thing now seems... for Lizzie to marry Duveneck.' And in the following January he wrote to his mother: 'I wish Lizzie would wed Duveneck!'

This was the time when he was writing *Washington Square*. Henry James was far too subtle a novelist simply to put real people into his novels, as D.H. Lawrence would do, or Aldous Huxley, but nevertheless the germ of three of his books was undoubtedly supplied by the Boott-Duveneck triangle. In all three—*Washington Square*, *The Portrait of a Lady*, *The Golden Bowl*—a rich and protective father has a vulnerable only daughter whose hand in marriage is sought by an unsuitable penniless suitor. Colm Tóibín, who has written brilliantly about James, points out that he changed Frank Duveneck, whom he saw as a penniless expatriate provincial, somewhat uncouth, into a handsome, penniless fortune hunter (*Washington Square*), into a timid expatriate collector (*The Portrait of a Lady*), into a penniless and untrustworthy Roman prince (*The Golden*

Bowl). Thus, when all differences have been taken into account and all space allowed for James's imagination, Francis and Lizzie Boott provided the inspiration for Dr Sloper and Catherine, for Gilbert Osmond and Pansy, for Adam Verver and Maggie.

The house that Gilbert Osmond lives in is very clearly based on the Villa Castellani at Bellosguardo. In chapter xxij of *The Portrait of a Lady*, we read 'The villa was a long, rather blank-looking structure', with 'a front upon a little grassy, empty, rural piazza which occupied a part of the hill-top.' The same villa had already figured in *Roderick Hudson*.

Early in 1886, Lizzie Boott finally agreed to marry Frank Duveneck. She wrote to a friend: 'It has been a long affair for years. The thing was given up entirely at one time but on meeting again we find that the old feeling is not dead and we are going to take up life together as we did not like it very well apart... I could not have been separated from my father after all these long years together. As it fortunately happens, this will not be. We shall all live together, most happily, I hope.' They were married in March, Francis Boott having made Frank sign a prenuptial contract specifying that Lizzie's fortune was to remain hers, 'for her sole and separate use forever'.

On 25 May Henry James wrote to his friend Boott: 'I wonder, my dear Francis, whether you will do me rather a favour. My excellent friend Constance Fenimore Woolson is in Florence and I want to pay her your compliment and administer to her some social comfort. The finest satisfaction I can confer upon her will be to ask you to go and see her, at Casa Molin, the old Pension Barbensi, on the Lung'Arno, which you will know.' Boott immediately called on Miss Woolson and she was made welcome at the Villa Castellani, where in due course she rented some rooms in one of the wings. Her great uncle James Fenimore Cooper had lived near Bellosguardo, and as we have seen the Villa Castellani had figured in two of James's novels, *Roderick Hudson* and *The Portrait of a Lady*.

In 1886 James took a flat in De Vere Gardens, London. That year he published his essay on John Singer Sargent, as well as *The Bostonians* and *The Princess Casamassima*. After the publication of the latter, he decided he would take another trip to Italy, to see the Boott-Duvenecks and Miss Woolson, known as Fenimore. He asked his Bellosguardo friends to keep his arrival secret, as he had no intention of being drawn into the Florentine social whirl. He did however let Vernon Lee know his plans: 'I shall come and see you very quickly,' he told her, 'though I mean to lodge, for sweet seclusion's sake, in one of [the] grand old villas.' On the subject of grand old villas, by the bye, he has this interesting passage: 'Their extraordinary largeness and massiveness are a satire on their present fate. They weren't built with such a thickness of wall and depth of embrasure, such a solidity of staircase and superfluity of stone, simply to afford an economical winter residence to English and American families.'

He arrived in Bellosguardo on 8 December. It had been agreed that he would sublet the nearby Villa Brichieri from Fenimore during December, since she still had her rooms in the Villa Castellani until the end of the year. He and Fenimore would be on their own in Bellosguardo, as the Duvenecks were down in the city, where Lizzie was expecting a baby. It is not clear what their feelings were for one another, though it seems likely that Fenimore was in love with James. For his part he had no intention of marrying anybody. In the new year she moved in, and they both carried on their literary work in different parts of the Villa Brichieri, James working on his novella *The Aspern Papers* and Fenimore on her novel *East Angels*. The fact of sharing a villa with a woman was excruciatingly embarrassing for James, and he attempted to disguise the situation in his correspondence, going so far as to describe Fenimore as 'a neighbour'. The Villa Brichieri has a famous terrace with a double view, north-east towards Florence and south-west towards Scandicci. Lizzie's baby arrived on 18 December and was christened Frank; now a proud grandfather, Francis Boott promptly tore up the prenuptial agreements he had made Duveneck sign. Everyone, it seems, was happy.

In 1888 James published *Partial Portraits*, and more tales. For Carnival that year the old Jewish ghetto of Florence, deserted and about to be demolished, was prettily decorated like a Chinese town, with gardens, pagodas and *tableaux vivants*. In March Duveneck's portrait of his wife Lizzie, and Lizzie's watercolour of the Villa Castellani, were both accepted by the jury of the Paris Salon. On the very day the jury met, Lizzie fell ill in Paris. She died of pneumonia on 23 March, and Frank was prostrated with grief. For James, Lizzie's 'sudden death was an unspeakable shock': he had known her from her childhood.

The tomb that Duveneck made for his wife's grave in the Allori cemetery in via Senese is very loosely based on the one that Jacopo della Quercia made for Ilaria del Carretto in Lucca Cathedral. There are several copies of Lizzie's tomb in the United States.

In the spring of 1890 Henry James was again in Florence, where his raging toothache required emergency dental care. (That year the equestrian monument to Vittorio Emanuele II was inaugurated in what was to become piazza della Repubblica; it was later moved to piazza Vittorio Veneto, at the entrance to the Cascine.) His old friend Dr William Wilberforce Baldwin discovered him in an hotel nursing his jaw, and insisted that James come and stay with him in his apartment on the corner of via Palestro and corso d'Italia. 'I have never been so be-doctored', James wrote. He paid a sad nostalgic visit to Bellosguardo, but Fenimore was no longer living there and the place filled him with melancholy. His sister Alice died in 1892.

In January 1894 Miss Woolson either fell or jumped to her death from her Venetian palazzo: James was appalled, and could not face going to her funeral, though later he went to Rome to visit her grave. In 1895 his play *Guy Donville* was booed off the London stage. Two years later he settled in Lamb House, Rye, and wrote *The Turn of the Screw* and *What Maisie Knew*.

What sort of a person was Henry James? William Faulkner called him 'one of the nicest old ladies I ever met', but the adjective that springs to mind is 'pompous'. Edith Wharton recalled how she was once driving with him to Windsor, when her chauffeur said he could not find the King's Road. They stopped to enquire the way, and a gormless old man appeared, staring at the car. James said: 'My good man, if you'll be good enough to come here, please; a little nearer, so.' The old fellow reluctantly approached, and James proceeded: 'My friend, to put it to you in two words, this lady and I have just arrived from Slough; that is to say, to be more strictly accurate, have recently *passed through* Slough on our way here, having actually motored to Windsor from Rye, which was our point of departure; and the darkness having overtaken us, we should be much obliged if you would tell us where we are now in relation to the High Street, which, as you of course know, leads to the Castle, after leaving on the left hand the turn down to the railway station. In short, my good man, what I want to put to you in a word is this: supposing we have already (as I have reason to think we have) driven past the turn down to the railroad station (which in that case, by the way, would probably not have been on our left hand, but on our right), where are we now in relation to...' At this point Mrs Wharton interrupted: 'Oh, please do ask him where the King's Road is.' 'Ah! The King's Road? Just so! Quite right!

Can you, as a matter of fact, my good man, tell us where, in relation to our present position, the King's Road actually *is*?' The old man replied, 'Ye're in it'.

He was also rather greedy. In Bresse his landlady set before him some of the local butter, saying coquettishly: '*Nous sommes en Bresse, et le beurre n'est pas mauvais.*' James recalled: 'It was the poetry of butter, and I ate a pound or two of it; after which I came away with a strange mixture of impressions of late Gothic sculpture and thick tartines.'

But James could on occasion behave with kindness and delicacy. Henry Dwight Sedgwick recalled: 'Poor old Godkin had had a stroke. At breakfast Henry James made some ordinary remark—"Pass me the butter", perhaps. Godkin thought it a joke and laughed aloud. Henry James at first was puzzled; then (and it was one of the nicest things I ever saw) began to smile as if hesitating to laugh at his own wit, and finally joined in Godkin's hearty laugh.'

In 1907 James made his final trip to Italy. He spent most of the time— seventeen days—in Rome, where he visited Fenimore's grave, though it appears that he also saw Florence for one last time. However, his diligent biographer Leon Edel confesses: 'We have no record of this final visit.'

At various times John Singer Sargent had made sketches of Henry James, but he always felt that 'it was impossible to do justice to a face that was all covered in beard like a bear.' The beard and moustache finally disappeared in 1900.

For James's seventieth birthday in 1913, a group of friends subscribed for a formal portrait of him by Sargent. Artist and novelist had about a dozen sittings, chatting companionably the while. Writing to his brother, James said: 'One is almost full-face, with one's left arm over the corner of one's chair-back and the hand brought round so that the thumb is caught in the arm-hole of one's waistcoat, and said hand therefore, with the fingers a bit folded, entirely visible and "treated".' James was delighted with the result: 'in short a living breathing likeness and a masterpiece of painting', he said. He was allowed to keep the portrait for his lifetime, after which it went to the National Portrait Gallery. In 1914 he began war work, visiting hospitals, etc., and he became a British subject in 1915. This was to show solidarity with Britain, before America had joined in the War. He was appointed to the Order of Merit early in 1916, a rare distinction, and he died on 28 February that year believing he was Napoleon.

The Irish playwright OSCAR WILDE (1854-1900) was fired with a desire to see the masterpieces of the Italian Renaissance by the writings of Walter Pater and the lectures of John Ruskin, while he was still an undergraduate at Magdalen College, Oxford. His opportunity came in 1875 when he and his friend William Goulding took a continental holiday with Professor the Revd John Pentland Mahaffy, a thirty-eight-year-old advocate of 'Greek love' who was himself something of a renaissance polymath. They visited Ravenna—which that year happened to be the set subject for the Newdigate Prize poem, a prize that Oscar duly won—and Florence, where like many other people he was captivated by the church of San Miniato and by the view from it over the city. Presumably the little party stayed in a pensione, but we do not know which. His somewhat sentimental poem 'San Miniato' was later published in a Dublin magazine. In a letter to his father he describes visits to the Biblioteca Laurenziana and to the Etruscan collections in the former convent of Sant'Onofrio, and also to the Chapel of the Princes at San Lorenzo, which (as we should expect) he very much liked, especially admiring the 'walls built entirely of gorgeous blocks of marble, all inlaid with various devices and of different colours, polished like a looking-glass. Six great sarcophagi of granite and porphyry stand in six niches: on top of each of them a cushion of inlaid mosaic bearing a gold crown'. (Later in life, he remembered these Florentine sarcophagi when he said to his young friend Robert Ross: 'Ah, Ross! When we are dead and lying in our porphyry tombs, and the trump of the Last Judgement is sounded, I shall turn and whisper to you "Robbie, Robbie, let us pretend we do not hear it".') In a later letter to Lord Houghton, he mentions 'the beautiful coloured bust of the Rajah of Koolapoor', which he must have seen at the far end of the Cascine (though he misremembered it as coloured). This is the monument to Rajaram Chuttraputti of Kolhapur, who died aged twenty-one in Florence in 1870: his body was cremated according to the Hindu rites at the confluence of two rivers, the Arno and the Mugnone. Wilde began writing 'A Florentine tragedy', in cod renaissance verse, but never finished it: it was given a first performance at Palazzo Davanzati in 2009. A poem called 'By the Arno' presents a picture of dawn breaking over Florence: 'The oleander by the wall / Grows crimson in the dawning light... '.

It is said that in Florence Wilde experienced a deep desire to join the Roman Church, but resisted it; the eponymous hero of *The Picture of Dorian Gray* experienced a similar desire, 'but he never fell into the error of arresting his intellectual development' by giving in to it; on his deathbed in the shabby Hôtel d'Alsace, rue des Beaux-Arts, Paris, Wilde was indeed received as a Catholic, by Fr Cuthbert Dunne on 9 November 1900.

Before that he returned to Florence in May 1894, in the company of Lord Alfred Douglas. Oscar's long-suffering wife Constance had hoped to accompany her husband to Florence, but he much preferred to spend the time there with 'Bosie' Douglas. The visit was clandestine, and Wilde travelled separately via Paris. In Florence he saw a good deal of Bernard Berenson, who disliked Bosie and regarded him as a corrupting influence. Berenson tried to warn Wilde against Douglas, but his advice was rejected with 'elegant insolence'. Oscar remarked: 'Bernard, you forget that in every way I want to imitate my Maker, and like him I want nothing but praise.' Berenson's lover Mary Costelloe introduced Oscar to Vernon Lee's half-brother, Eugene Lee-Hamilton: 'It was a great success. Oscar talked like an angel, and they all fell in love with him, even Vernon Lee, who had hated him almost as much as he had hated her. He, for his part, was charmed by her', Mary wrote. (In her 1884 novel *Miss Brown*, Vernon Lee had caricatured Wilde as an 'elephantine person' with a 'flabby, fat-cheeked face'). Wilde also visited Walburga Lady Paget, at the Villa Torre di Bellosguardo, and he signed the visitors' book at Frederick Stibbert's house. On their last day in Florence, Oscar and Bosie bumped into André Gide, and were able to offer him the use of the flat overlooking the Arno that they had taken for a month, since they were leaving after only a fortnight.

In Florence Wilde's memory was long kept alive by his friends Reggie Turner and Ada ('Sphinx') Leverson.

VERNON LEE (real name Violet Paget, 1856-1935) was born in France but from 1878 lived in Florence with her parents. The Paget family moved from via Solferino to via Garibaldi. Vernon Lee lived at Villa Palmerino, in the valley of the Affrico at Fiesole, from March 1889 until her death. She was an intimate childhood friend of the great American artist John Singer Sargent (who painted a magnificent portrait of her in 1881, and later sketched her androgynous likeness), and her home became a chief

Oscar Wilde   *Vernon Lee portrayed by Sargent*

meeting ground for the intellectuals and aesthetes of Anglo-American and Florentine society. She wrote her first book aged sixteen or seventeen, and a very brilliant one it was, on Italian music in the eighteenth century. In 1893 Henry James described her as 'by faraway the most able mind in Florence.' Virginia Woolf wrote approvingly: 'She picks her feet up.' A founding member of the Society for the Protection of Old Florence, Vernon Lee wrote a long letter to *The Times* on 15 December 1898 about the disembowelling of the city centre (the Old Market and the Jewish ghetto). The centre, she said, 'a unique ensemble of medieval streets and lanes—was not cleared or ventilated, or drained or otherwise sanitated, but simply swept off the face of the earth, not a trace remaining in the group of commonplace and inappropriate streets, and the ostentatious and dreary arcaded square [now piazza Repubblica] which arose on its site'. This letter had a good effect and helped to create a climate of opinion that prevented further destruction before it was too late. She was assisted in her efforts by many foreign residents, such as John Temple Leader, Frederick Stibbert and Adolf von Hildebrand. In less than three months she collected more than 11,000 signatures to stop the demolition.

After years of neglect, Vernon Lee's literary reputation is now steadily rising, and each year sees conferences and seminars devoted to her work.

The castle of Acciaiuoli at Montegufoni

In 1909 the eccentric garden-designer Sir GEORGE SITWELL (1860-1943) wrote to his elder son, a schoolboy at Eton: 'My dearest Osbert, You will be interested to hear that I am buying in your name the castle of Acciaiuoli (pronounced Accheeyawly) between Florence and Siena... The castle is split up between many poor families, and has an air of forlorn grandeur. It would probably cost £100,000 to build today. There is a great tower, a picture gallery with frescoed portraits of the owners, from a very early period, and a chapel full of relics of the Saints. There are the remains of a charming old terraced garden, not very large, with two or three statues, a pebblework grotto and rows of flowerpots with the family arms on them. The great saloon, now divided into several rooms, opens into an interior court where one can take one's meals in hot weather... We shall be able to grow our own fruit, wine, oil, even champagne!... The purchase, apart from the romantic interest, is a good one, as it returns five per cent. The roof is in splendid order, and the drains can't be wrong, as there aren't any. I shall have to find the money in your name, and I do hope, my dear Osbert, that you will prove worthy of what I am trying to do for you, and will not pursue that miserable career of extravagance and selfishness which has already once ruined the family. Ever your loving father, George R. Sitwell.' When he first saw it, Sir George was struck

Sir George Sitwell

Osbert Sitwell

by the castle's immense size, for it was almost twice as big as Renishaw, his ancestral pile in Derbyshire. Montegufoni—the hill of the screech-owls—had five separate courtyards, three massive terraces, a chapel, a limonaia big enough to contain over 200 ancient lemon trees in terracotta pots, a grotto, some 100 rooms (there were originally seven houses until they were knocked together in the fifteenth century), a hall somewhat larger than the Great Hall at Hampton Court, and a central bell tower modelled on the campanile of Palazzo Vecchio in Florence. It had been built by the Acciaiuoli family, who like the Sitwells (though several centuries earlier) had made their money out of steel. However, not only was the castle falling to bits but it was occupied by no fewer than 297 squatters, together with their sheep, goats, hens and other livestock. Sir George was totally undismayed and decided on the spot to buy it. The asking price of £4,000 was most reasonable, though of course it would cost many times that to restore.

A few years later OSBERT SITWELL (1892-1969) went to Florence and visited his property, the Acciaiuoli castle at Montegufoni, for the first time. There he found his father already installed, happily issuing a stream of directions to the workmen and generally setting about restoring the place, accompanied by his enormous English butler, Henry Moat. In one of the volumes of his autobiography Osbert wrote: 'While we wandered through the high, cool rooms of the great house or, if it were not too hot, along the three sun-baked decks of the garden, Henry would be unpacking an ample luncheon of cold chicken, and Angelo Masti, the peasant in charge, would hurry in with a large, flat, cylindrical cheese, the pecorino of the neighbourhood, with a basket of figs and late peaches, tinged with green, and grapes, all still warm from the sun—some of these being of the kind called *fragole*, the small, plump, blue grapes, so different from others in their internal texture, and in their taste, which recalls that of the wood strawberry, that they might be fruit from the planet Mars or Venus—or a huge flask, covered in dry, dusty rushes, of the excellent red wine of the Castle itself... And these things to eat and drink would be placed on a table covered with the coarse white linen used by the contadini, under a ceiling painted with clouds and flying cupids, holding up in roseate air a coat of arms, a crown and a Cardinal's hat.'

Sir George used to say to his visitors: 'I must ask anyone entering the house never to contradict me or differ from me in any way, as it interferes with the functioning of my gastric juices and prevents my sleeping at night.' He invented a revolver for shooting wasps, and wrote a book on the history of the two-pronged fork. He was very fond of the Middle Ages, and passed his life in a medieval dream.

IV

THE EARLIER TWENTIETH CENTURY

BY THE TIME the new century dawned, Florence and the rest of Tuscany had been part of the kingdom of Italy for some four decades. King Vittorio Emanuele II of Savoy, the first sovereign of united Italy, was succeeded in 1878 by his son Umberto I. Together with his wife Margherita of Savoy, Umberto visited Florence in November 1878, on the eve of one of several attempts to assassinate him. Known to his friends as the 'Re Buono' and to his enemies as the 'Re Mitraglia', Umberto was murdered at Monza by an anarchist on 29 July 1900. The regicide, Gaetano Bresci, 'hanged himself' in his cell the following year.

The forty-six-year reign of Umberto's son Vittorio Emanuele III saw two world wars, universal male and female suffrage (in 1912 and 1945 respectively), the decline and fall of the Liberal State (1900-1922), the resolution of the Roman question (1929), and the rise and fall of Fascism (1925-1943). Vittorio Emanuele died some eighteen months after the final extinction of the kingdom of Italy, which by his cowardly flight to Brindisi in September 1943—leaving the army without orders—he had made inevitable.

In the halcyon years before the First World War, the British and American 'residential community' in and around Florence numbered some 35,000 and there were sizeable self-contained groups—Iris Cutting called them archipelagos—of French, Germans, Russians and Poles. The heart of the Anglo-American community was however a relatively small group of rich people who all knew each other; in alphabetical order one might mention Arthur and Hortense Acton at Villa La Pietra, Bernard and Mary Berenson at Villa I Tatti, Lady Sybil Cutting at Villa Medici, Herbert Percy Horne in via de' Benci, Henry Labouchère at Villa Cristina, Ada Leverson in various hotels such as the Porta Rossa in via Porta Rossa, Charles Loeser at Villa Gattai, Violet Paget at Villa Palmerino, Walburga Lady Paget at the Torre di Bellosguardo, Janet Ross at Villa Poggio Gherardo, Sir George and Lady Sitwell at the Castello di Montegufoni, Charles Augustus Strong at Villa Le Balze. They all visited each other's villas, spending many hours of each day drinking tea or cocktails and passing on tittle-tattle. Whether it was because the Anglo-Americans were better organised, or noisier, or more numerous, the fact is that the artistic and intellectual importance of the German and French communities was rather overshadowed. Of the 2,300 entries in the loan journal of the Gabinetto Vieusseux for 1897, some 1,100 are those of Britons or Americans. The Austrian journalist Sigmund Münz wrote: 'If the level of conversation about a city may be taken as a decisive factor, then Florence is more European than many a metropolis. Society here has an international cachet... Anglicised Italians and Italianised Britons are a common phenomenon.' In his last remark Münz may have had in mind the phrase '*inglese italianizzato, diavolo incarnato*', which was by no means a compliment. It was an expression that was perhaps first applied to the sanguinary Sir John Hawkwood.

The New York novelist and garden designer EDITH WHARTON (née Jones, 1862-1937) travelled with her family in Europe between the ages of four and ten. They visited France, Germany, Spain and Italy, and little Edith— known as Pussy—acquired a good knowledge of European languages. Her rich parents are said to have given rise to the expression 'keeping up with the Joneses'. They settled in Florence in 1870, and returned to the United States two years later. She wrote a certain amount as a teenager, though she was not encouraged to do so by her family, who thought authorship vulgar. Edith came out as a debutante in New York in 1879, and six years later she married Teddy Wharton, a Bostonian friend of her brother's, who was twelve years older than she. In the later 1880s and throughout the 1890s they travelled in Europe, mostly in Italy. She met Bernard Berenson in 1903 and they intensely disliked one another. That year on 17 March she wrote to her friend Sally Norton from the Hotel Bristol in Florence: 'We did not reach here until last night and Miss Paget [Vernon Lee] has such a prodigious list of villas for me to see near here and is taking so much trouble to arrange expeditions for us that I think we shall have to stay here longer than I expected.' The result of Edith's exploration of the villas was published in 1904 as *Italian Villas and their Gardens*, with dreamy illustrations by Maxfield Parrish. Of Florence she wrote: 'For centuries Florence has been celebrated for her villa-clad hills. According to an old chronicler, the country houses were more splendid than those of the town, and stood so close-set among their olive orchards and vineyards that the traveller "thought himself in Florence three leagues before reaching the city".' Of the Medici she explained: 'It is perhaps owing to the fact that Florence was so long under the dominion of one all-powerful family that there is so little variety in her pleasure-houses. Pratolino, Poggio a Caiano, Cafagiuolo, Careggi, Castello and Petraia, one and all, whatever their origin, soon passed into the possession of the Medici.' She has this to say about Boboli: 'The most important, if not the most pleasing, of Tuscan pleasure-gardens lies within the city walls. This is the Boboli garden, laid out on the steep hillside behind the Pitti palace. The plan of the Boboli garden is not only magnificent in itself, but interesting as one of the rare examples, in Tuscany, of a Renaissance garden still undisturbed in its main outlines.' Her novel *The House of Mirth* appeared the following year. Edith crossed the Atlantic no fewer than sixty times. Her husband Teddy Wharton was a depressive, and his mental condition deteriorated to the point that he was declared incurable in 1908; five years later she divorced him. In September 1909 in Paris Edith again met Berenson, and this time she liked him very much. They did not fall in love, but they developed a close and intimate platonic friendship that lasted for the rest of Edith's life. They would joke about their first meeting: Berenson told his wife 'I used to make her scream with laughter as I gave her a truthful account of our first impressions of her.' Villa I Tatti became her spiritual home, and she visited it every year. In Paris during the Great War, the frenchified Edith worked heroically on behalf of refugees and the homeless, and for her war work she was made a chevalier of the Legion of Honour. Her novel *The Age of Innocence* (1920) won the Pulitzer Prize for Fiction in 1921. In May 1937 she visited her old friend and collaborator Ogden Codman, at his beautiful house at Grégy-sur-Yerres,

Edith Wharton

Ada Leverson

and there she suffered a heart attack. Ogden wrote: 'It was all very complicated and upsetting. Her almost last words as she left in the ambulance were, "This will teach you not to ask decrepit old ladies to stay." I should think it will!' She lingered on for a couple of months, enjoying smelling the summer flowers and feeding the fish in a pond, and died on 11 August at her Pavilion Colombe at St-Brice.

The novelist and wit ADA LEVERSON (née Beddington, 1862-1933) was part of the circle of Oscar Wilde, who called her 'Sphinx'. She was an extremely loyal friend to him at the time of his trials for homosexual offences and was one of the few people who met him on his release from H.M. Pentonville Prison on 19 May 1897 ('Sphinx, how marvellous of you to know exactly the right hat to wear at seven o'clock in the morning to greet a friend who has been away!'). She once wrote of somebody at a fancy-dress party as 'wearing a grape-skin and a bunch of leopards'. Among her most admired novels are *The Limit* (1911), *Tenterhooks* (1912) and *Love at Second Sight* (1916). Latterly she spent long periods in Florence, usually living in hotels, and in the 1920s she was a familiar sight tottering along the via Tornabuoni. Sphinx was excessively devoted to the Sitwell siblings, especially to Osbert. She was good friends with Dr Giovanni Battista Roatta, the suave and humane physician to the English-speaking community in Florence. Harold Acton was always friendly to her, presumably because she was a living link to Wilde, but her dottiness put many people off. She sent him a great many barely legible letters and postcards in the 1920s and early 1930s. In July 1931 Harold reported to his mother that the poor old Sphinx had fallen out of the upper berth in her wagon-lit and had broken several ribs. In June 1933 Dr Roatta wrote to her ('Of course I have not forgotten you dear Sphinx, there is only one Sphinx in this world and one does not forget her'), commiserating with her about her broken wrist. Ada Leverson died in Florence on 30 August 1933. In the following February Harold bumped into Osbert in Peking, who gave him 'a Sitwellian account of Sphinx's death.'

The American collector and connoisseur CHARLES LOESER (1864-1928) was born in Brooklyn, son of a German Jewish immigrant who had arrived in the US with nothing in 1853 and had built up a large and flourishing dry-goods business. From the year 1881 until it was sold in the 1950s, the Frederick Loeser & Company Department Store in Brooklyn occupied a whole block bound by Elm Place, Fulton, Bond, and Livingston Streets. Charles Loeser showed not the slightest interest in taking on the family business, preferring the life of a scholar and connoisseur, and his father seems to have been perfectly happy to support him, in fact he was proud to have a non-working son, a sort of bumble bee rather than a drone.

At Harvard in the 1880s he studied art under Charles Eliot Norton, and he later went back there to take a master's degree in philosophy. Harvard brought him into contact with future art scholars and collectors such as Grenville Winthrop (a 'snob and a cold patrician' who assembled a collection of over 4,000 works of art), William Randolph Hearst and Bernard Berenson, but as his college friend the philosopher George Santayana observed: 'In America, he floated on the surface and really lived only in the international world of art, literature and theory.' Like a character out of a Henry James novel, Loeser was able to use his private income to gain access to the wider social and cultural environment of Europe, and to indulge his passion for collecting. After a period in Berlin he settled in the 1880s in Florence, where he lived first in a turreted house in via Lambertesca, Palazzo Bartolommei. At one time he shared a flat with Bernard Berenson on the lungarno Acciaiuoli. He met and married Olga Kaufmann. A little later he bought and restored the Villa Torri di Gattaia, on the viale dei Colli, which is now the International School of Florence, at viuzzo di Gattaia no. 9. It was in Florence that 'Carlo', as he liked to be called, felt really at home and where he decided to spend the rest of his life. Mabel Dodge, who lived at the Villa Curonia, knew him before the First World War and she recorded her impressions of him in her memoirs: 'Loeser lived in studious discomfort. His rooms were meagrely furnished with a few perfect pieces of quattrocento noce; cinquecento was far too ornate for him after a youth in Brooklyn... Himself—he looked like a terrier, with one ear up and the other down, so cocked was one eyebrow and so snapping his red-brown canine eyes. Head on one side, his long face creased into deep lines, he often laughed spasmodically and satirically with rarely a genial laughter. It was more like a suspicious kind of mirthful bark. His voice had a timbre like cat-gut scraping the strings of a bass viol, but his speech was very scholarly.' That was Mabel Dodge, later Luhan, and it was she who observed that for many foreign collectors in Florence, persons and objects had an approximately equal value.

In an article that Harold Acton wrote for *Apollo* in October 1965 about his own father's collection, he recalls some of the collectors he used to meet as a child at Villa La Pietra and then says: 'Pre-eminent among these for connoisseurship, Charles Loeser inhabited various medieval towers—he had what might be called a "tower-complex"—before he built his sprawling villa of La Gattaia... Horne, Loeser and my father often visited antique shops together; sometimes they made exchanges. With Loeser, for instance, my father exchanged a terracotta figure on a horse for a *Madonna and Child Enthroned* by the so-called Magdalen Master (1270-1275), a picture which was vastly improved by judicious cleaning... Loeser and Horne shared a preference for early Tuscan furniture of extreme austerity as though they wished to mortify the flesh... there was something slightly comical about Loeser's ecstasies over a severe monastic chair or bench, for he had the caressing voice of a voluptuary. Loeser was wont to write standing at a stiff lectern, which was, to him, an aid to composition. I regret I was not old enough to record his entrancing disquisitions, of which his published writings give no idea.' In his memoirs, Harold

Acton echoed Mabel Dodge's aphorism in speaking of Charles Loeser: 'His taste, like Herbert Horne's, was fastidiously selective and exclusive. Art interested him far more than human beings.'

Like the dealer Egisto Fabbri, Loeser was an important early collector of Cézanne, and the music room at the Villa Gattaia was adorned with several paintings by the modernist Provençal master. In that room the Léner Quartet used to play, surrounded by Loeser's Cézannes. Speaking of Florence before the first War, Harold Acton said in his memoirs that '...the Guelfs and Ghibellines had been replaced by rival schools of art-historians. Between Berenson, Horne, Loeser and Perkins one never knew what fresh crisis had arisen. It must have been a difficult time for hostesses.' (The fourth collector Acton mentions is F. MASON PERKINS, 1874-1955, who was an American protégé of Berenson's, based in Siena and Lastra a Signa, and who eventually bequeathed his pictures to the Sacro Convento in Assisi.)

The Italian Quattrocento style responded perfectly to Loeser's taste for elegant simplicity, although in practice his collecting covered a much broader field. On his death in New York in 1928 he left some 260 Italian drawings to Harvard, his choice Cézannes to the President of the United States and thirty works of art—paintings and sculptures—to his adopted and much-loved city of Florence. These are now displayed on a mezzanine in Palazzo Vecchio, as one descends the stairs from the Sala del Giglio, and many of them have been beautifully restored by the foundation set up by Loeser's granddaughter, Philippa Calnan. They include Bronzino's *Portrait of Laura Battiferri* (Bartolomeo Ammanati's wife); the *Portrait of Ludovico Martelli* attributed to Pontormo; paintings by Pietro Lorenzetti and Piero di Cosimo; sculptures by Tino di Camaino, Jacopo Sansovino, Benvenuto Cellini, Giambologna; some excellent examples of old Tuscan furniture; and the bronze *écorché* horse that Loeser always insisted was by Leonardo himself.

In 1906 the versifier and art historian HERBERT PERCY HORNE (1864-1916) bought the Palazzo Corsi (possibly by the great fifteenth-century architect Simone del Pollaiuolo known as Cronaca) on the corner of via de' Benci and corso dei Tintori, which he set about restoring most beautifully and patiently. Born in 1864, he was the son of Horace Horne and

Charles Loeser

Herbert Horne

Hannah Louisa Gibson. His father is said to have been an architect, but is described as a 'railway carrier' on Horne's birth certificate, and by the writer Arthur Symons as 'a regular bad lot, dissipated, shady, cruel and selfish'. Herbert Horne had a younger sister called Beatrice, a gifted musician, and also a brother called Louis who was a psychiatric case and died in an asylum. Horne attended Miss Moore's day school in Kensington, where his interest in art was encouraged by the critic Daniel Barton Brightwell. Next he went to Kensington Grammar School, and immediately afterwards he was articled to one of his relatives, a surveyor called George Vigers; but Horne was a clever fellow and soon moved to the studio of Arthur Heygate Mackmurdo, becoming a partner in 1884 at the remarkable age of twenty. Mackmurdo wrote 'I took him into partnership very soon... Horne was endowed with extraordinary creative power; a power extremely versatile and impatient to prove itself in any direction which opportunity might offer.' Mackmurdo was an admirer of Ruskin and William Morris, and he founded the Century Guild which published the journal *The Hobby Horse*. The aim of the Century Guild was to 'render all branches of Art the sphere no longer of tradesmen but of the artist'. *The Hobby Horse* was modelled on *The Germ* (1848), the publication of the Pre-Raphaelite brotherhood. Mackmurdo and Horne were co-editors of the first edition in 1884 then Horne took over between 1886 and 1892. Horne had read Walter Pater's *The Renaissance*, and had much admired it, just as Oscar Wilde had, and Pater's sumptuous and highly wrought prose was his introduction to Italian renaissance art. As a matter of fact Horne saw a good deal of Oscar Wilde from 1886 to 1891, and he also knew the Rosettis, Walter Pater himself, and the poet W.B. Yeats. Horne was a leading light of the Rhymers' Club, which met at the public house 'Ye Olde Cheshire Cheese' in Fleet Street, or else at the Café Royal, and he published some slim volumes of verse. He made friends with Bernard Berenson in 1888, the year when the demolition of the old Jewish ghetto began. In the following year Horne visited northern Italy (together with the painter Frederic Shields, who was thirty years older than he) to work on a commission for Mrs Gurney, a rich and pious old widow from a Quaker banking family. Horne's diary of this trip has interesting Florentine descriptions of, for example, Benedetto da Rovezzano's carvings in Santi Apostoli and for the tomb of St John Gualbert (then in the Bargello, now at San Salvi). Benedetto went to England and worked for Henry VIII: the sarcophagus he carved for Cardinal Wolsey was set aside after Wolsey's disgrace and some 300 years later was used to contain the corpse of Admiral Nelson in St Paul's Cathedral.

Horne lived with his parents. In 1892 he left the studio of the architect Mackmurdo to strike out on his own, 'designing buildings in a vaguely Quattrocento style': his masterpiece, the chapel of the Ascension in the Bayswater Road, partly modelled on Santa Maria delle Grazie in Pietrasanta, was destroyed by enemy action in 1940, as were several of his other London buildings. The interior of the Ascension chapel was frescoed in vaguely Trecento style by the painter Frederic Shields, Horne's travelling companion in northern Italy.

Horne was back in Tuscany in 1894, commissioned by the publisher George Bell to write a book about Botticelli. In July 1897 he was squiring Mary Costelloe (the future Mrs Berenson) and the art historian Julia Cartwright Ady round the Ospedale della Scala in Siena. He advised on art collections for the Metropolitan Museum in New York and dealt with many private collectors, including J.P. Morgan. In January 1899 he entered into a formal contract with Berenson to dispose of Italian works of art on the London market, for a half share of the profits, though he and Berenson later fell out. In 1901 he published the first of two extraordinarily brilliant articles on Botticelli in *The Burlington Magazine*. He moved permanently to Italy in 1904, having sold his collection of English watercolours to Edward Marsh for £2,400: this amazing collection included works by Gainsborough, Cozens, Romney, Blake, Cotman and Turner. He published annotated editions of Vasari's life of Leonardo, and of Condivi's life of Michelangelo. He purchased Palazzo Corsi in 1906. In 1908 his great book on Botticelli was published by George Bell: it was entitled *Alessandro Filipepi Commonly Called Sandro Botticelli Painter of Florence*, and was entirely designed by Horne, who provided neither chapter headings nor index, and printed only 240 copies; it was admiringly reviewed by Roger Fry in the *Burlington Magazine*. Fry consulted Horne about various art-historical matters. In 1908 he wrote to his mother Lady Fry: 'I have had a very busy time of going round the various dealers and learned a great deal from my cicerone and host Mr Horne, who knows Florentine art as no one else does, and has made a wonderful collection without ever giving large prices.'

In more recent times John Pope-Hennessy praised Horne's book on Botticelli as 'the best monograph in English on an Italian painter', and Fritz Saxl called Horne 'perhaps the most accomplished historian of art whom this country has ever produced.' William Rothenstein recalled Reggie Turner saying: 'Dear Herbert Horne! poring over Botticelli's washing bills—and always a shirt missing!' The year his book appeared Horne sold his *Entombment* predella by Giovanni di Paolo to Henry Walters of Baltimore. As a little boy Harold Acton had been told that Horne had two rows of teeth and was always trying to peer into Horne's mouth to see if this was true, but could never quite manage it.

Despite or perhaps because of his austere lifestyle, Horne's health deteriorated. Aby Warburg visited the dying Horne in 1915, noting that he lived in the smallest rooms of the palazzo in great discomfort. Horne on his deathbed repaired his friendship with Berenson, according to a letter from Mary to her brother Logan. And in a letter to her sister in April 1916 the tender-hearted Mary claimed to have 'got Horne to make his will yesterday, and to make provision for his faithful servant. He has left... his Palace and works of art here to the State for a Museum... It wrings my heart to go and sit with him. His mind is softening and he clings to me. I've known him for 31 years.' Horne died a few days later aged fifty-two, and was buried at the Allori cemetery in via Senese. Mary wrote: 'The

Horne Museum

funeral was rather awful, the assistants being mainly Sods (excuse the word) and dealers, with B.B. and Loeser (they might be called dealers), myself and one or two Museum officials of grubby aspect. He was buried near his mother in the Protestant Cemetery. Herbert Trench went with us, and hardly had the earth been sprinkled on him than Trench said to me "I wrote a great Poem yesterday, 40 lines… I'll send you a copy", while Loeser was saying "The next time I marry, it shall be to a Deaf Mute". So everybody's life resumed its only very slightly ruffled flow.'

Horne's monument is, apart from the book on Botticelli, the Horne Museum in via de' Benci, stuffed with paintings, sculpture, majolica, glass, coins, tapestries and furniture belonging to the fifteenth, sixteenth and seventeenth century. When I first came to Florence in 1971 Harold Acton advised me to go and see it, and also the Stibbert Museum, and I have been repeating this advice to visitors to Florence ever since. Among the paintings that Horne collected are the famous panel of *St Stephen* attributed to Giotto, Dosso Dossi's *Allegory of Music*, a fragment of a cassone by Filippino Lippi showing Queen Vashti leaving the city of Susa, and the diptych of the *Madonna col Bambino* and *Cristo in pietà* which is attributed to Simone Martini. The creation of such a collection is a remarkable achievement given Horne's comparatively slender financial resources. Kenneth Clark, who thought Horne 'perhaps the most distinguished man to be omitted from the Dictionary of National Biography', wrote in his autobiography: 'Horne had made an excellent collection with very little money. When someone asked him for a photograph of one of his pictures he said "Why have a photograph? It's cheaper to buy an original".'

ROBERT LANGTON DOUGLAS (1864-1951) was an art dealer and connoisseur who bought and sold, but he was also a good art historian and later a museum director. Denys Sutton, writing in *Apollo*, called him a 'notable and endearing figure...in every way a *galantuomo*.' As a child in Sheffield, Langton Douglas attended the Collegiate School which was near Ruskin's St George's Museum, where hung the lovely *Madonna and Child* attributed to Verrocchio and now in the National Gallery of Scotland. Langton Douglas's father was the vicar of St Stephen's in Sheffield, and to please him Langton Douglas took Anglican orders after studying at New College Oxford. He was not really suited to being a clergyman as he was very amorous and had several families concurrently. In 1895 he became the Church of England chaplain in Leghorn, in 1896 in Genova and in 1897 (very briefly) in Siena. In Florence he gave courses on Dante, Savonarola, Machiavelli and Michelangelo, and he travelled around a good deal. At the end of the decade he had to return to England where Archbishop Temple wisely allowed him to resign from the Anglican Church. By now art history was his main interest and he cut his teeth by producing an annotated edition of the famous *History of Italian Painting* by J.A. Crowe and G.B. Cavalcaselle, that had been first published in the year of his own birth. Then in 1900 Langton Douglas wrote a good book on Fra Angelico, whose career he convincingly reinterpreted, and two years later a *History of Siena*, based on the archival sources made available to him by his friend Alessandro Lisini, director of the State Archives in Siena. Langton Douglas loved Sienese art and praised Duccio highly, believing that his neglect in favour of Giotto was all Vasari's fault.

The *History of Siena* was well received, except by Berenson and his friends. Berenson's protégé F. Mason Perkins gave the book a hostile review in the *Burlington Magazine* for April 1903, unwisely questioning

Langton Douglas's attribution of the *Rucellai Madonna* to Duccio. Berenson himself wrote an anonymous review, remarking patronisingly that the author was capable 'of good work in subjects where finesse or taste are not needed.' Langton Douglas stirred things up with an article on Sassetta in the very next issue of the *Burlington*: it was called 'A Forgotten Painter', it correctly ascribed the beautiful *Mystic Marriage of St Francis* in the Musée Condé of Chantilly to Sassetta, and it provocatively pointed out that Sassetta is not even mentioned in Berenson's *Central Italian Painters*. Berenson was enraged, especially as he considered himself an authority on Sassetta, whose lovely *St Francis in Glory* he had bought from an ignorant shopkeeper in 1900. He responded with two long articles on Sassetta, not deigning to mention Langton Douglas by name.

The feud between Robert Langton Douglas and Bernard Berenson smouldered on for decades, throughout their art-dealing careers, occasionally throwing out showers of sparks. It is the sort of regrettable behaviour that is very common among art historians, who belong to one of the more malicious professions. They were both good looking, they were both attractive to women and attracted by them, and they both loved to hold court. Langton Douglas was the more fluent writer, Berenson the smoother conversationalist.

In 1904 Langton Douglas set himself up as a dealer, buying on behalf of J.P. Morgan and of the Kaiser Friedrich Museum in Berlin. He was responsible for some of the major acquisitions of the Metropolitan Museum in New York: in 1910, for example, he bought for the museum from Mrs Arthur Severn two magnificent figures by Giovanni Pisano which had once been owned by Ruskin.

In 1914 Langton Douglas dyed his hair and pretended he was forty rather than fifty, so as to enlist in the army as a private soldier. He was given a commission in the Army Service Corps and managed to continue his art dealing. When Sir Hugh Lane went down to the bottom of the sea with the *Lusitania*, Langton Douglas was appointed to succeed him as director of the National Gallery of Ireland. During the seven years of his directorship he sold the Gallery a number of his own pictures, works by Guardi, Beccafumi and Antoniazzo Romano: inevitably he was criticised for this, though the prices he awarded himself seem to have been not excessive, and after all he was improving the Gallery's holdings. But he would probably not get away with that today. In 1928, when he was sixty-four, Langton Douglas suddenly married a young woman in her twenties, Jean Stewart. This was his third wife. In the 1930s he was received as a Catholic, and after the deaths of his earlier wives he was able to marry Jean in a church.

By a previous marriage he had a pretty daughter called Claire, who married the famous reclusive author of *Catcher in the Rye*, J.D. Salinger.

Langton Douglas very much admired Luca della Robbia, and was in his turn admired by John Pope-Hennessy, who wrote a good monograph on Luca.

In the Second World War he again tried to join up—having perhaps dyed his hair again—but was told he was far too old. He produced a convincing theory about Sienese art: in the 1430s, when Sienese artists were unable to visit Florence because of the wars, artistic fashions changed and according to Langton Douglas the young Sienese artists became very nationalistic. They turned against all the modern trends that were then popular in Florence, which is why fifteenth-century Sienese painting is so archaic. Langton Douglas strongly believed that art historians should always examine the political context and that they should be capable of using documentary sources to this end.

In New York the firm of Duveen rather kindly made the ageing Langton Douglas a consultant. In 1951, aged eighty-seven, he came back to Tuscany and was installed in the convent of the Blue Sisters in Fiesole, to his great delight. He made up his quarrel with Bernard Berenson (just as Horne had done on his deathbed), he enjoyed eating *pastasciutta*, and he was taken to the cinema once a week by Arthur Acton, who would drive over from La Pietra to pick him up in his comfortable car. John Pope-Hennessy was alarmed to see how extremely old Langton Douglas had become, but his mind was still very active, and his comment to Pope-Hennessy was 'My, how you've aged!'

BERNARD BERENSON (1865-1959) came to Florence in December 1890 with his lover Mary Costelloe (née Pearsall Smith), whom he had met in London in 1888. Raised in a Quaker family in Philadelphia, Mary had converted to Catholicism on the occasion of her marriage to Frank Costelloe; Bernard (originally named Bernhard Valvrojenski) had been raised in a Jewish family in Lithuania, but he too became a Catholic in February 1891. In

Robert Langton Douglas

Bernard Berenson

December that year Mary moved definitively to Florence and they settled into separate apartments on the lungarno Acciaiuoli.

Having emigrated from Lithuania to Boston at the age of ten, the brilliant and talented Berenson was educated at Harvard and was sent to Europe by a gang of rich and adoring Bostonians. Like 'a young Goethe', he could have done anything he wanted, and at various times he studied both astronomy and Sanskrit. Eventually he chose Italian painting as his field of study, adopting and adapting the methods of Giovanni Morelli, whose contribution to the study of painting he thought 'greater than Winckelmann's to antique sculpture or Darwin's to biology.' Mary became Bernard's pupil and under his supervision wrote a catalogue of the paintings at Hampton Court (1894); her share in his writings was far greater than has been realised until recently. The pair of them travelled extensively through Tuscany, Umbria, Emilia-Romagna, Le Marche and northern Italy, acquiring an unrivalled knowledge of Italian painting. Although he had thitherto been averse to acting on commission, in 1892 he took his first percentage on a painting by Piero di Cosimo, and it gave him a taste for it. In the following year he met the collector Theodore Davis from Newport, Rhode Island, and became a consultant for him; around the same time he started advising Isabella Stewart Gardner from

Boston; he collaborated with Otto Gutekunst of Colnaghi. Later, his secret agreement with the exceedingly successful dealer Joseph Duveen would bring him abundant riches. In 1896 Bernard published his highly original *Florentine Painters of the Renaissance*, which had a great success and was saluted by William James as the first attempt to apply 'elementary psychological categories to the interpretation of higher works of art.' Six years of hard work led to the publication in 1903 of *The Drawings of the Florentine Painters*. On 29 December 1900, the now widowed Mary Costelloe married Bernard Berenson, first civilly in the Palazzo Vecchio in Florence and then religiously in the chapel at Villa I Tatti, Ponte a Mensola, which they had just rented from John Temple Leader. I Tatti became Berenson's home for the next fifty-nine years, and there he held his little court for intellectual and artistic types; there he collected his remarkable library of some 50,000 volumes and some 170,0000 photographs; he also assembled a collection of Asian art, and of Italian paintings, including the *Madonna and Child* by Domenico Veneziano and the *Glory of St Francis* by Sassetta. In 1907 they purchased the property from Temple Leader's heir, Lord Westbury, and set about making improvements. MARY BERENSON (1864-1945) was fat, untidy, fond of her family, intellectually superior; she called everyone 'thou' in the Quaker manner, like her sister Alys, who married the mathematician and philosopher Bertrand Russell. In April 1909 she noted in her diary that she had sacked the Italian architects and had engaged Cecil Pinsent to work on I Tatti. Earlier, she had introduced him to her young protégé Geoffrey Scott. Pinsent lived in constant terror of Berenson, whose sharp eye was continually detecting faults in the workmanship: 'Cecil is terribly afraid of BB, and BB is gloomy and preoccupied', as Mary wrote to her family in May 1909. According to Nicky Mariano, both Berensons seemed to feed on visitors, irrespective of how nice or interesting they were. They were happy to talk about people for hours, their manners and their scandals, 'so long as these throw light upon the chase of human nature, fit quarry for a noble curiosity', as Percy Lubbock noted. Mary once told Kenneth Clark that no poem in the English language meant more to her than Thomas Hood's line 'Give me new faces, new faces; I've seen all the old ones a thousand times o'er', while even the delicate-stomached Berenson 'could swallow the toughest American bore.'

During the Second World War Berenson had to go into hiding, but

Berenson outside the Villa I Tatti

with the Allied victory he was able to return to an undamaged Villa I Tatti. There Berenson's miniature court resumed its clockwork pattern, supervised by his beloved Nicky Mariano, now that Mary was dead. He worked undisturbed in his study in the morning; he came down to luncheon at one precisely, alert and immaculately dressed, 'his delicate blue veined hands looking as fragile and translucent as porcelain' (Alan Moorhead), talking eloquently and courteously to his guests, usually about politics and almost never about art, eating little and drinking less; he took a rest after luncheon, reappearing precisely at half past five for tea; after tea he walked in the gardens; dinner in black tie started promptly at eight; after dinner Nicky Mariano read to him in one of several languages.

Berenson's reputation grew and grew. He died in his bed at I Tatti on 6 October 1959; his body was wrapped in an ivory-coloured cashmere shawl, and a Crucifix was laid on his breast; the funeral cortège, winding its way to the little church of San Martino a Mensola, stretched for nearly half a mile.

In April and May of 1910 the Staffordshire novelist ARNOLD BENNETT (1867-1931) was in Florence, working on his ambitious new novel *Clayhanger*, a coming-of-age story set in the Midlands. He had already published *Anna of the Five Towns* (1902), *The Grand Babylon Hotel* (1902) and *Old Wives' Tale* (1908). However much he wrote in a day, and it was generally a lot, he always managed to keep up his almost daily journal, which by the end of his life amounted to over a million words. It provided raw material for his fiction. As a young man Bennett had trained as a painter, and his imagination was highly visual. Here is his description of borgo Santa Croce, which runs from via de' Benci towards the basilica: 'A narrow street containing 6 or 8 ancient palaces, in which doctors, lawyers, etc, live like birds in the side of a precipice. You go up to one of the *porte-cochères* [a 'porte-cochère' is a doorway wide enough to admit a carriage] and see a courtyard, and groined roofing, and iron-work, with glimpses of vast stairs and upper corridors and storeys, all grim and stony. At top of some stairs a double iron gateway. Each palace may be inhabited by perhaps a dozen families, or more. The rooms must be very high and dark, according to the windows, as there are only ground-floor and two storeys in these lofty palaces. Projecting eaves are always a striking feature. The ground-floor windows are far off the ground, and barred.'

Bennett was a gourmet—the delicious *Omelette Arnold Bennett* (made with butter, eggs, cream, cloves, parsley and smoked haddock fillet) is named after him—and in his diary he gives an admiring description of a highly professional Florentine chef: 'We dined... at Lapi's, in the cellar in the Via Tornabuoni. Here the cooking is done in full view of the audience. Each dish prepared specially for each client. All by one man. About 35, dark, personable, extraordinarily quick and graceful. If he left his recess for a moment to go upstairs he would slide down the rail to come back again. Charcoal stove. He blew it up constantly with a fan. Sparks fl[ew]. He put on charcoal with his hand... He would fan with one hand and stir with another. He made an omelette in a moment: very quick his gesture in turning it over like a pancake, in the pan. Very careful and slow in making our coffee... All professional conversation very loud, and constantly going on. Things not in stock, such as ham, sent for and brought down in a paper... Graceful leave-takings from all the personnel as we left. Bill and tip 8½ lire for 3 people.' (Lapi's had opened in 1879, in the cellars of Palazzo Antinori, with its entrance in the lane that runs from via Tornabuoni towards the Croce al Trebbio.)

In the centre of Florence Bennett saw 'crowds of men, some in very amusing fur coats, at the north-west corner of Piazza della Signoria.' He greatly admired Palazzo Strozzi, and made up his mind to write an article about it. At the Uffizi he deplored the 'irregularity' of the rooms, which confused him, and he felt that the collection of paintings deserved to be housed 'if not with grandeur and splendour, at any rate with a certain conventional distinction', like the Wallace Collection in Hertford House.

He describes getting lost on the left bank of the Arno: 'I left the girls [Marguerite and Pauline Smith, who were in his party], and crossed the P[onte] Vecchio, and took a steep street to the left [presumably Costa San Giorgio], aiming at S. Miniato. But I never reached it. I got quite lost and *désorienté*. Ultimately, after insisting for long that I ought to turn to the left, I admitted that I must turn to the right, and then I came to the Porta Romana, and got a little rural omnibus to the Duomo.' (After Costa San Giorgio he must have walked along via San Leonardo as far as the viale, and then turned right for Porta Romana instead of left for San Miniato.) Another day he went to piazza Peruzzi, which impressed him deeply, 'partly for its Gothicness, and partly because of the streets round it whose curves (Baedeker) show the lines of the old Roman amphitheatre'—as indeed they do. Later he returned by night to the area, and found it full of prostitutes: 'they were a sinister-looking lot, but they suited the architecture', was his enigmatic comment.

Like many another writer, Bennett found the atmosphere of the city conducive to literary creativity: 'Florence is certainly an ideal place to write a novel in, at least to arrange your ideas for a novel in.' Also, he was responsive to the beauty of Florentine art: 'Every day you come across new quantities, enormous quantities, of really high class work. The Donatello etc. things, the M. Angelo tombs, and the MSS. in the Library adjoining, would alone make the reputation of a city. And they are a mere trifling item in the total.'

Bennett's last words, spoken to his companion Dorothy Cheston, were: 'Everything has gone wrong, my girl.'

Arnold Bennett

Norman Douglas

The travel writer NORMAN DOUGLAS (1868-1952), who was of Scottish-Austrian ancestry, came to live in Florence in February 1917, and stayed on and off—he travelled a good deal—for twenty years, until his sudden departure from Italy in May 1937, following a sexual scandal involving an underaged child, unusually in this case a girl. Edward Hutton, another travel writer, introduced Norman Douglas to Reggie Turner, the loyal friend of Oscar Wilde, who had arrived in Florence at about the same time. Reggie thought Norman 'A mixture of Roman emperor and Roman cab driver.' Norman was a master of English prose—his celebrated novel *South Wind* had appeared in 1917—and in some respects fastidious and patrician, but he was also a heavy drinker and an unrepentant paedophile. Evelyn Waugh described *South Wind* as 'the only great satirical novel of his generation.'

Douglas had a flat on the lungarno delle Grazie which at some stage he shared with his louche friend Giuseppe Orioli, the publisher of the famous Lungarno series. Norman had taken a vow never to enter a church (which certainly handicapped him as a writer of guidebooks), and he resolutely avoided the houses of the rich. Although he was great friends with Harold Acton, despite their thirty-five-year difference in age, he never set foot in the Villa La Pietra. What he liked to do was meet his gossipy friends in the inexpensive restaurants he patronised: Betti's, or Cesare's, or Fusi's in via Condotta. The friends included Reggie Turner, Pino Orioli and Richard Aldington. Norman wrote: 'I never go to the British Institute. It is crowded day and night with frowsy old pension-cats, who occupy all the chairs and read, each of them, five newspapers at the same time.'

Ian Greenlees, a director of the British Institute, recalled that Reggie Turner once persuaded Norman to take tea—a beverage and a meal that he detested—at the villa in Fiesole of an English lady who was longing to meet the author of that amusing novel *South Wind*. All the way there in the taxi Norman grumbled. Hardly had he entered his hostess's draw-ing-room when he suddenly remembered a pressing appointment and left. Later, Reggie found him sitting alone in a bar.

Norman Douglas had been born in the Vorarlberg in Austria in 1868. When he was eight his widowed mother remarried, and sent him to school at Uppingham in England, which he hated. He completed his edu-cation at the Karlsruhe Gymnasium, which was unsupervised and where the schoolboys gambled, drank and kept mistresses.

He then joined the British diplomatic service. His short career ended in St Petersburg in 1895, when one of his two Russian lovers fell preg-nant—the first of many sexual scandals that constellated his existence. Douglas fled to Italy, bought a house in the bay of Naples, and married his first cousin Elsa, whom he came to loathe. By 1904 he was divorced and no longer sexually interested in adults.

To his wife's consternation, he won custody of their two sons, Archie and Robin. His family fortune having collapsed, he worked for the *English Review* and wrote a series of books, including *Siren Land* (1911) about Capri, and *Old Calabria* (1915) about the toe of Italy. In 1916, the year his former wife burned to death in an hotel fire, he was arrested for kissing a boy in South Kensington Underground station, and jumped bail. He fled to the Mediterranean. In the following year his masterpiece *South Wind* was published, a novel about pagan goings-on in Capri, renamed 'Nepenthe'.

Ian Greenlees, director of the British Institute from 1958 to 1980, was a great friend of Douglas's from the early 1930s, and a MS he wrote is a good source of information about the older man. Ian recalled: 'Norman liked to be completely independent and did not want to be troubled with a res-ident servant. He preferred eating in restaurants; avoiding hospitality in private houses was almost a fetish with him. "If I lunch in a Cinquecento villa my dear, I can hardly send my food back to the kitchen if it is badly cooked," he would say. "Can you imagine — being pleased if I tell him the pasta has been cooked too long, or the veal is too tough? No, my dear, it is much better to be free and eat on your own. If I get bored, how can I leave if I am a guest? That is why I make it a rule never to accept invitations to private houses".'

From the autumn of 1932 Ian Greenlees often joined Norman for a meal in one of the simple Florentine restaurants that he favoured, such as Fusi in via Condotta. Ian wrote: 'His habit was to head for the inner dining-room, choose his table and then study the menu carefully while exchanging light banter with Pomponio the waiter, or with the proprietress whose brother was the chef. Norman would invariably walk into the kitchen, examine what there was to eat and advise the chef as to how he wanted his pasta and his meat cooked. If the meat was undercooked or tough, if the pasta was not al dente, Norman would raise his voice and tell the waiter it was uneatable and must be sent back. He believed it was your duty to show an interest in what you ate; otherwise, the proprietor would think you didn't care and serve you with whatever slop he wanted to be rid of.'

Ian did not share all of Norman's strong opinions, but he greatly admired him for holding them. He was aware of what we might call Norman's cultural limitations, and in a pamphlet he wrote for the British Council in 1957 he noted: '[Douglas] had little knowledge of Italian literature, and in fact read little Italian poetry, and few novels or short stories. Neither was he interested in Italian painting nor in any kind of painting. Although he lived for many years in Florence, he was prone to dismiss the architecture and pictures there with a contemptuous tone of voice as so much "Cinquecento"'. Many other writers have noted Norman's amusing use of this shorthand term for everything pretentious and meretricious in the worshippers of high Italian culture: 'Isn't that rather Cinquecento, my dear?' he said to Nancy Cunard, when she suggested going to see some renaissance art. There is a fine line between robustness of mind and philistinism.

Norman used to say that a good luncheon was worth all the Benozzo Gozzolis in the world. He did however have scientific interests, and in his twenties he published monographs on such subjects as *The Herpetology of the Grand Duchy of Baden, The Pumice Stone Industry of the Lipari islands* and *On the Darwinian Hypothesis of Sexual Selection*. He also made a collection of London children's street games, and another of obscene limericks, complete with pseudo-scholarly notes and a geographical index.

At the outbreak of the First World War the cosmopolitan character of Florence to a large extent disappeared, as huge numbers of foreigners left the city.

An exception to this trend was Oscar Wilde's loyal friend REGINALD TURNER (1869-1938), who settled in Florence in mid-January 1915. His flat was at no. 5 viale Carlo Alberto (now viale Giovane Italia, near the Nazione building). He had first visited the city during a tour of Italy in 1898, and had fallen in love with it. He was very sociable in Florence, for unlike Norman Douglas he did not avoid smart houses and in general was very fond of tittle-tattle. Reggie paid court to Lady Ida Sitwell of Montegufoni, the impossible mother of Edith, Osbert and Sacheverell, and he would spend hours on end listening to the outpourings of Ada Leverson, 'the Sphinx', who had become very dotty in her old age and lived in a series of hotels such as the Porta Rossa in via Porta Rossa. He was an assiduous frequenter of the weekly At Homes of the Marchesa Torrigiani, an outspoken American who had married into the local nobility. He moved into a flat in the viale Milton (destroyed in the last War). Reggie loved to be visited in Florence by his literary friends, who included Arnold Bennett and H.G. Wells, and he was immensely proud when someone sent him a postcard from London addressed to 'Reggie Turner, Florence' and it was immediately delivered. He had written a dozen or so novels, but none of them was any good. He was one of those witty people—Maurice Bowra was another—whose wit evaporated the moment he picked up his pen.

Harold Acton recalled: 'Reggie was never allowed to slip demurely into middle age. He was continually being embarrassed. One day as he was walking down the Via Tornabuoni, Ronald Firbank, whose mere voice made Reggie wince, rushed upon him from a flower-shop and covered him from head to toe with lilies.' Firbank was exceptionally effete, even by the standards of expatriate Florence, but Reggie was rather sad to learn from the composer Lord Berners of Firbank's lonely death in Rome, in 1928, aged only thirty-nine.

One of the celebrated foreign expatriates whom Reggie did not especially take to was Bernard Berenson. As early as 1910 he had introduced
an unflattering caricature of Berenson in one of his novels, *Count Florio
and Phyllis K*, which has a character who is a tiresome art expert called
'Barnard Barnardsohn.' It may be that Reggie shared the view of Norman
Douglas, who told the young Ian Greenlees to avoid Berenson, 'an old
fraud dripping with culture'. The collector and dealer Martin Birnbaum
records in his autobiography, *The Last Romantic*, an incident involving
Turner and Berenson, whose remarkable collection at Villa I Tatti had
been assembled partly as the result of Berenson's profitable secret partnership with the phenomenally successful art dealer Joseph Duveen.
Birnbaum relates how one day Berenson showed Turner 'the literary
and artistic treasures stored in Tatti, but as they wandered through the
halls lined with books and paintings, not a word escaped Turner's lips.
This piqued BB, and finally he insisted on knowing what Turner really
thought of his pictures. After a good deal of prodding, the Englishman
whispered hesitatingly: "Oh, I think they are simply Duveen!"'.

Somerset Maugham wrote that Reginald Turner 'was on the whole
the most amusing man I have known... Reggie liked an audience, though
he was quite content with one of three or four, and then he would take a
theme, and embroider upon it with such drollery that he made your sides
so ache with laughter that at last you had to beg him to stop.'

After Norman's enforced departure from Florence Reggie carried on
much as before, though depressed by the deteriorating political situation
and by his own failing health. When Somerset Maugham and his partner
Gerald Haxton passed through Florence in the spring of 1938, on their
way from the Far East to the south of France, they were alarmed to find
Reggie very frail.

He was extremely well looked after by his devoted servants, the
Romellis, to whom he left the residue of his estate, after a bequest to Pino
Orioli. When Reggie's beloved pet dog was run over on the viale and
killed, the Romellis bought him a replacement puppy and gave it to him
as a surprise on his return from a visit to Venice. (I had this information
from the granddaughter of Reggie's servant Leone Romelli.)

Listen to the world-weary Richard Aldington, writing in the 1950s in
his memoir about Norman Douglas and Pino Orioli: '...in the summer
of 1938 I received a letter from Reggie, rather a sad one, congratulating

Reginald Turner

W Somerset Maugham

me on the birth of my daughter, "the only real immortality". I did not know then how far gone he was with that dreadful disease, cancer of the tongue. Suddenly came a telegram from Pino to say Reggie was dead, whereupon I cabled him money to lay a wreath from me on Reggie's tomb—I think the only one I have ever sent in my life. Why did I waste money on what I thought then and still think an absurd superstition and a profanation of beautiful flowers, which should be devoted to the feasts of youth and the courtship of women?' Aldington answers his own question by recalling how Reggie, when he could ill afford it, had paid for a wreath at Oscar Wilde's funeral in Paris in 1900, how he had deserved well from the republic of letters, how he had stood loyally beside the fallen hero, etc.. The result was that Reggie's grave in the Allori cemetery was adorned with flowers sent by both Aldington and Orioli, bearing the very same wording as had been used at that other funeral, thirty-eight years previously.

The stammering, bridge-playing novelist and short-story writer WILLIAM SOMERSET MAUGHAM (1874-1965) came to Florence fairly often in the 1930s. At one stage he had been secretary to C.K. Scott Moncrieff. He was friends with Arthur Acton, the owner of Villa La Pietra and father of the writer Harold and the painter William. Maugham's 1941 novel

Edward Hutton

Mabel Dodge Luhan

Up at the Villa, a tale of adultery and suicide, is supposedly based on the Acton home; during the War Arthur asked his son Harold to send him a copy of it, presumably so he could show it off to the other guests at the Hôtel des Trois Couronnes in Vevey, Switzerland, where he and his wife Hortense were holed up for the duration. It was Maugham whose boasting about the rarity of first editions of his novels prompted Reggie Turner to remark, with reference to the dismal sales of his own novels, 'it's my second editions that are very rare!' Max Beerbohm in describing Reggie's wit remarked that he was not very responsive to other people's humour. The comment rather worried Reggie, who asked Maugham if he thought it were true. 'I didn't want to hurt his feelings, so I said "Well, Reggie, you never laugh at any of my jokes". He blinked... & puckered up his... face, and with a grin replied "But I don't think they're funny".'

The future travel writer EDWARD HUTTON (1875-1969) first came to Italy aged twenty-one in 1896, having just inherited £5,000 on coming of age. He fell in love with the country and devoted the rest of his life to studying and expounding its culture and history. In 1898 he married Charlotte Miles, and around 1901 they rented the so-called Casa Boccaccio at Corbignano, not far from the homes of Bernard Berenson and Janet Ross. During the First World War Hutton supplied the Allied intelligence with detailed lists of the monuments to be protected from enemy attack. In 1917 he was one of the founders of the British Institute of Florence, a cultural centre with a language school and a library that still exists. That year he was appointed to the Ordine della Corona d'Italia in recognition of his war work, and in 1924 he was given a gold medal by the British Academy for his contribution to Italian studies. Among his Florentine writings are *Florence and Northern Tuscany with Genoa* (1907), *Country Walks about Florence* (1908) and *Florence* (1952).

The socialite and memoirist MABEL DODGE LUHAN (née Ganson, 1879-1962) came to live in Florence in 1905, having married her second husband Edwin Dodge in the previous year. They settled into his Villa Curonia, at Arcetri, and set about restoring it. He had trained as an architect at MIT and later at the École des Beaux Arts in Paris. Unfortunately the house and its beautiful formal garden 'drank money', and rich as Edwin was he began to feel the strain of improving Villa Curonia. Mabel described her life there in her racy autobiography *Intimate Memories* (1933) and in *European Experiences* (1935). In the latter book she wrote about the largest room in the house: 'The Gran' Salone! How achieved it was! It satisfied something in me. The way the light came in past the full golden red curtains, the way the logs burning in the fireplace threw a golden light on the dark oak floor, the glimpses of the Italian hills one caught from outside the loggia, framed between the pale stone columns... like the backgrounds in early Florentine paintings.' Arthur Acton was friends with Mabel Dodge and in 1910 he organised a recital by the celebrated actress Eleonora Duse at the Villa Curonia.

In October 1901 the future novelist EDWARD MORGAN FORSTER (1879-1970) arrived in Florence with his formidable mother Lily. He was twenty-two and they were on what he later called 'a very timid outing' from England to Italy. Forster and his mother stayed briefly at the Albergo Bonciani in via de' Panzani, but they did not like it—no doubt it had no view—and they soon moved to the Pensione Simi, at no. 2 lungarno delle Grazie. (Later on in their Italian travels he tripped up and broke his arm, which was put into a cast, so that his mother had to wash him like a baby, after

EM Forster

Virginia Woolf

which she commented that he looked cleaner than usual.) Like Lucy Honeychurch in *A Room with a View*, Forster was dismayed to discover that his landlady at the Pensione Simi had a Cockney accent. He wrote to the musicologist E.J. Dent: 'She scatters Hs like morsels and calls me "the young gentleman".' Altogether Forster stayed three times in Florence, in 1901, 1902 and 1903, and during those years he spent only a few months in Italy as a whole, so it is remarkable that his novels *Where Angels Fear to Tread*, set in Tuscany, and *A Room with a View*, set partly in Florence, have effectively defined the region and the city for English readers. Indeed, he did not spend much longer on the Indian sub-continent and yet managed to produce his acknowledged masterpiece, *Passage to India*. There is a pattern to be discerned here: Hippolyte Taine spent only eight days in Florence, yet was able to write about the city in sparkling and knowledge-able fashion.

The future novelist VIRGINIA WOOLF (1882-1941) came to Florence in April 1904 and stayed at the Palace Hotel, which as I have recently discovered was in Palazzo Lanfredini on the lungarno Guicciardini. At that time she was Virginia Stephen, being the daughter of the critic, mountaineer and biographer Leslie Stephen, who had died just two months previously. On the 25th Virginia wrote to her cousin Emma Vaughan ('Dearest Toad'): 'We have been here for a fortnight: it is a lovely place, just not lovelier than Canterbury, I think—but I don't know. The view from Fiesole, the country round Fiesole, San Servasio [*recte* San Gervasio] etc., is almost more beautiful than anything I have seen. I won't write a dissertation on the Italian landscape because I know it would bore you. It is an amusing pretence to leave England by going to Florence (grammar all wrong).' She thought Italy was 'degenerate tho' beautiful', and rather smugly added: 'Thank God, I say, that I was born an Englishwoman.'

Five years later she was back again in Florence and wrote about it to Madge Vaughan (the original of Sally Seton in *Mrs Dalloway*), from the Hotel Manin in Milan: 'We spent a fortnight in Florence, and Nessa and Clive [her sister and brother-in-law] are staying on till the end of the month. We had a tremendous tea party one day with Mrs Ross. She was inclined to be fierce, until we explained that we knew you, when she at once knew all about us—our grandparents and great uncles on both sides. She certainly looks remarkable, and had type written manuscripts scattered about the room. I suppose she writes books. There were numbers of weak young men, and old ladies kept arriving in four wheelers; she sent them out to look at her garden. Is she a great friend of yours? I imagine she has a past—but old ladies, when they are distinguished, become so imperious. Lina Waterfield also came in for a moment, but I hardly spoke to her. She has beautiful eyes. The garden, though it rained, was wonderful; I could fancy you wandering about in it, and eating un-ripe oranges. Florence was lovely—more lovely than seems possible. We used to wander about along the river at all hours; or sit and bask on the hills.' Lina Waterfield, one of the founders of the British Institute, was the niece and ward of fierce old Janet Ross.

In 1933 Virginia Woolf published *Flush: a Biography*, her enjoyable life of Mrs Browning's Spaniel. For the latter part of the book she was able to draw on her Florentine memories. She described how Flush 'threaded his path through main streets and back streets, through squares and alleys, by smell. He nosed his way from smell to smell; the rough, the smooth, the dark, the golden. He went in and out, up and down, where they beat brass, where they bake bread, where the women sit combing their hair, where the bird-cages are piled high on the causeway, where the wine spills itself in dark red stains on the pavement, where leather smells and harness and garlic, where cloth is beaten, where vine leaves tremble, where men sit and drink and spit and dice—he ran in and out, always with his nose to the ground, drinking in the essence; or with his nose in the air vibrating with the aroma. He slept in this hot patch of sun—how sun made the stone reek! he sought that tunnel of shade—how acid shade made the stone smell! He devoured whole bunches of ripe grapes largely because of their purple smell; he chewed and spat out whatever tough relic of goat or macaroni the Italian housewife had thrown from the balcony—goat and macaroni were raucous smells, crimson smells... Nor was his sense of touch much less acute. He knew Florence in its marmoreal smoothness and in its gritty and cobbled roughness. Hoary folds of drapery, smooth fingers and feet of stone received the lick of his tongue, the quiver of his shivering snout. Upon the infinitely sensitive pads of his feet he took the clear stamp of proud Latin inscriptions. In short, he knew Florence as no human being has ever known it; as Ruskin never knew it or George Eliot either. He knew it as only the dumb know. Not a single one of his myriad sensations ever submitted itself to the deformity of words.'

The modernist Irish novelist JAMES JOYCE (1882-1941) spent even less time in Florence than did Sir Walter Scott. In the summer of 1908 he and his companion Nora Barnacle, and their two small children Giorgio and Lucia, returned by train from Rome to Trieste, breaking their journey in the Tuscan capital. This was his only visit. Joyce had a terrible hangover— no doubt a splitting headache and a tongue like the inside of a parrot's cage—, as he had been drinking in Rome with some low-life characters (bowsies, they would be called in Dublin), who had robbed him. He had had a month's salary in his pocket-book, which they snatched while he was fumbling with it. At this stage he had not yet published anything except for the poems of *Chamber Music*, but had been teaching languages in Trieste, until he found a slightly more lucrative post as a clerk in Rome. Joyce intensely disliked Rome and the Romans, and evidently could not wait to get back to Austrian-ruled Trieste.

The novelist and Nobel laureate HARRY SINCLAIR LEWIS (1885-1951)

James Joyce   *Harry Sinclair Lewis*

came to Florence during a European tour in 1921, when he witnessed the beginnings of Fascism. He wrote to his father: 'I came down here just at the tail end of the four-day strike and street-rioting (seven killed and scores wounded) which followed clashes between the Fascisti and Communisti [*sic*]. The so-called Communisti are workmen, union men, very few of whom are really socialists at all; and the Fascisti are a kind of American Legion, but much more violent.' He was known as 'Red' Lewis, partly because of his political opinions and partly because of his curious boiled-looking complexion. In 1930 he became the first American to win the Nobel Prize in Literature, at the age of forty-five. On another visit to Italy he described Mussolini as 'a flabby faced, hard-jawed, mad-eyed fanatic.'

He was back in Florence early in 1949, and was introduced by the Revd Sturgis Riddle to Bernard Berenson. Lewis found the famous art expert to be 'gay, approachable, suave, amusing, welcoming, and he knows almost as much about literature, American and British and French, as he does about trecento art.' For his part Berenson found Lewis to be unexpectedly presentable, with his 'fine blue eyes', having heard all sorts of rumours about his slovenly habits and heavy drinking.

From Florence Red wrote to his friend Ida Kay: 'I have more people here now whom I feel I know intimately than I do in Massachusetts and New York put together.' He found the Anglo-Florentines to make up 'an enchanted colony in an enchanted town and the king of it all is B.B. [Bernard Berenson].'

In November 1949 in Assisi, Lewis met the half-Polish Alexander Manson, who worked for the Thomas Cook travel agents. He was charmed by Manson and immediately took him on as his secretary, though to Lewis's friends Manson seemed an obvious fraud: he called himself Major Manson, although in the War he had only been a Sergeant-Major. And Berenson said of him: 'I know a Central European adventurer when I see one.' Lewis went with his new secretary to Florence, and rented the Villa La Costa on pian dei Giullari, beyond the Eyre Pazzi villa. It had been built by a local Fascist in the 1930s and its decoration was extremely kitsch. 'One entire wall of the main bathroom was glass, painted with images of tropical fish and backlit to give the illusion of an aquarium. Lewis loved to show people this room, chuckling with malicious glee', writes Red's biographer Richard Lingeman. Happy as he may have been among the expatriates, his health was deteriorating and his alcohol intake increasing. In 1950 Red entertained Evelyn Waugh and Harold Acton to a dinner that was a 'social and culinary failure.' He died in Rome in the following year, with Alex Manson at his side.

On a 'dark, wet, wintery evening' in November 1919, the Nottinghamshire miner's son DAVID HERBERT LAWRENCE (1885-1930) arrived by train in Florence. The city 'seemed grim and dark and rather awful on the cold November evening', which was Wednesday 19th. Hooded carriages glistened in the rain. From the station of Santa Maria Novella he headed for Thomas Cook's travel agency in via Tornabuoni, where a note was waiting for him from Norman Douglas, giving the name of a pensione in piazza Mentana. He had written in advance to Norman, who in these matters was always very reliable: 'Douglas has never left me in the lurch', said Lawrence. They had known one another from the days of the *English Review*, where Douglas had been assistant editor and had given the Lawrences a German-style luncheon to celebrate their marriage. Frieda Lawrence liked Norman because he could speak to her in her native German, but the two men were pleased to discover that they were

DH Lawrence

natural enemies. Lawrence thought Douglas a sybarite with a 'wicked red face and tufted eyebrows', while according to Douglas Lawrence was 'peevish and frothy'. At the far end of via Tornabuoni he reached the river, which was 'rushing like a mass of *café au lait*'. Muffled in his coat, with Douglas's note in his pocket, Lawrence made his way upstream along the lungarno. He had just passed the Ponte Vecchio, and was watching the night fall on the swollen Arno, when he saw two men approaching, one tall and portly, the other short and strutting, with a 'touch of down-on-his-luck about them both'. They turned out to be Norman Douglas and his friend Maurice Magnus. (It was about the ambiguous legacy of Magnus, after he took his own life in Malta in November 1920, that Lawrence and Douglas quarrelled.) At the Pensione Balestri, Lawrence was given a south-facing room with a beautiful view over the river, making him feel he was 'in a castle with the drawbridge drawn up.'

The travel writer Edward Hutton introduced Norman to Reginald Turner, Oscar Wilde's loyal old friend who had settled in Florence during the Great War, and Norman introduced Reggie to Lawrence.

Lawrence spent many evenings in Reggie's company, often in his flat in viale Milton. After a while he left Florence for Venice, but he was back again in the spring of 1921 and checked in once again to the Balestri. That very day Rebecca West, Reginald Turner and Norman Douglas all lunched together. As Rebecca wrote later: 'To each of us, different though we were in type, it seemed of paramount importance that we should go and pay [Lawrence] our respects at the first possible moment', and she describes how the three of them found him in his small room at the Balestri 'tapping away at a typewriter. Norman Douglas burst out in a great laugh as we went in, and asked him if he were already writing an article about the present state of Florence; and Lawrence answered seriously that he was. This was faintly embarrassing, because on the doorstep Douglas had described how, on arriving in a town, Lawrence used to go straight from the railway station to his hotel and immediately hammer out articles about the place, vehemently and exhaustively describing the temperament of the people. This seemed obviously a silly thing to do, and here he was doing it. Douglas's laughter rang out louder than ever, and malicious as a satyr's.'

What Lawrence had been tapping away at, that day in the Pensione Balestri, was the sixteenth and seventeenth chapters of his new novel *Aaron's Rod*, which came out in June 1922, a couple of months after Joyce's *Ulysses*. The novel's flute-playing hero arrives in Florence and enters, on a whim, the 'pension Nardini', 'a big old Florentine house, with many green shutters and wide eaves', in piazza Mentana. He is shown into 'a big bedroom with two beds and a red-tiled floor—a little dreary, as ever—but the sun was just beginning to come in, and a lovely view of the river towards the Ponte Vecchio, and at the hills with their pines and villas and verdure opposite.' The novelist and critic Francis King comments on this passage: 'It is a perfect evocation of a kind of pensione—Miss Godkin's, Miss Plucknett's, Mme Jenny Giachino's, the Jennings-Riccioli, the Levelis-Marke, the Bertelli-Scott—in which foreign visitors put up in the days before package tours and en suite facilities.' (When I first came to Florence in 1971, I stayed for a couple of months at the delightfully antiquated Pensione Antica in via Pandolfini—a vanished world.)

Lawrence had gone on ahead of his plump German wife Frieda von Richthofen, who joined him a few days later. He met her train at four o'clock in the morning and insisted on showing her the city straight away. Outside the station he hired one of the open carriages that were then so cheap and ubiquitous, and still exist today (though they are not cheap). Frieda described their night-time tour of Florence: 'I saw the pale crouching Duomo and in the thick moon-mist the Giotto tower disappearing at the top into the sky. The Palazzo Vecchio with Michelangelo's David and all the statues of men, we passed. "This is a man's town," I said, "not like Paris, where all the statues are women". We went along the Lungarno, we passed the Ponte Vecchio, in that moonlight night, and ever since Florence is the most beautiful town to me, the lily town, delicate and flowery.'

The two chapters of *Aaron's Rod* that are set in Florence contain vividly recognisable portraits of Norman Douglas, Reginald Turner and other Florentine expatriates. Douglas was most indignant when he saw the novel and wrote to a friend that it was 'a silly—really silly—account... Such tosh I never read.' To Edward Hutton he wrote about a 'droll description in Lawrence's latest book... He has also got Reggie into it, and others. Reggie is slightly annoyed, I fancy.' To Bryher (the penname of Annie Winifred Ellerman) Douglas wrote 'In fact, people in Florence are very furious with him for this book; he has put a lot of them into it, in a rather cat-like fashion.'

Norman Douglas appears in *Aaron's Rod* as the very outspoken and hard-drinking writer James Argyle; Reginald Turner appears as the spinsterish Algy Constable, blinking like a demented owl; the artist Collingwood Gee—or possibly the con-man Maurice Magnus—appears as 'Louis Mee'; and there is supposedly a character modelled on Bernard Berenson. In Florence the novel's flute-playing hero, Aaron, goes to an all-male party where these various expatriate characters are assembled. 'They all snapped and rattled at one another, and were rather spiteful but rather amusing.' James Argyle drinks too much, and talks very offensively in a clever imitation of Norman Douglas's conversational style, insulting Algy Constable who clucks and flaps and blinks. I can imagine that Reggie might have been annoyed at being presented as the butt of Norman's ill humour, but he can hardly have objected to Lawrence's vignette of his entertaining arrangements in the flat in viale Milton: 'The next day at Algy's there was a crowd. Algy had a very pleasant flat indeed, kept more scrupulously neat and finicking than ever any woman's flat was kept. So to-day, with its bowls of flowers and its pictures and books and old furniture, and Algy, very nicely dressed, fluttering and blinking and making really a charming host, it was all very delightful to the little mob of visitors. They were a curious lot, it is true: everybody rather exceptional. Which, though it may be startling, is so much better fun than everybody all alike.'

Annoyed as they may have been for a while, the Anglo-Florentines soon forgave Lawrence and indeed they were all delighted when he decided to come back to Florence, or rather to Scandicci, where he installed himself in the very rustic Villa Mirenda at San Paolo a Mosciano, and began writing *Lady Chatterley's Lover*. From Villa Mirenda Lawrence wrote to Dorothy Brett: 'I've not been in Florence for a fortnight. Then

I saw Reggie Turner. Like most people there he's going rather rapidly to pieces. Really, he's getting quite gaga! The town has a bad effect on one. I am glad to be in the country.' He was by that time mortally ill from the tuberculosis that would kill him before his forty-fifth birthday. While writing the novel, Lawrence would invite his friends over to the Villa Mirenda to listen to chapters of it read out aloud. There is a painting of Lawrence reading from the manuscript of *Lady Chatterley* to Reggie, Norman and Norman's friend Giuseppe Orioli, the bookseller and publisher of the famous Lungarno series. It was Orioli who later saw the first edition of *Lady Chatterley* through the press of the Tipografia Giuntina. Another person present on this particular evening was of course the artist, Collingwood Gee, who painted the picture from memory after Lawrence's death. I know nothing whatever about Collingwood Gee except for the remark by Compton Mackenzie that he was 'the most completely homosexual man I have ever met.' One cannot help thinking that this was a rather odd audience for the great English novel of heterosexual passion.

Lawrence was of course very serious about sex, whereas Douglas was giggly about it, and reported delightedly that *Lady Chatterley* was 'one of the filthiest books I have ever read.' Reggie on the other hand strongly disapproved of the novel's indecent language, which he thought a 'disfigurement of literature' and a 'wilful outrage on other people's feelings.' He was staggered at the book's eventual reception, writing to Edward Hutton that *Lady Chatterley* was 'selling like anything' in both the Giuntina and the pirated editions. 'I don't understand it, for I think it is a rotten book', he said.

Lawrence has an interesting passage on the dawn of Fascism: 'In the summer of 1920 I went north, and Florence was in a continual socialistic riot: sudden shots, sudden stones smashing into the restaurants where one was drinking coffee, all the shops suddenly barred and closed. When I came back there was a great procession of Fascisti and banners... It was the beginning of Fascism. It was an anti-socialist movement started by the returned soldiers in the name of Law and Order... Only another kind of bullying.'

In June that year Lawrence visited the Sitwells' castle of Montegufoni, and in a letter to his friend Mrs Otway he wrote: 'Sir G. collects beds... Room after room, and nothing but bed after bed. I said "but do you put your guests in them?"—Oh! he said. They're not to sleep in. They're museum pieces. Also gilt and wiggly-carved chairs. I sat on one. Oh! he said. Those chairs are not to sit in!—So I wiggled on the seat in the hope that it would come to pieces.' While he was in Italy, Lawrence made some superb translations of stories by Giovanni Verga, including 'Cavalleria Rusticana'. To his Nottinghamshire family he was known as 'Bert', but his cosmopolitan friends all called him 'Lorenzo'.

In August 1921 Lawrence and Frieda were lent a flat at 32 via de' Bardi. On 1 September Lawrence wrote to its owner: 'Dear Nelly Morrison: I had your letter yesterday. Everything goes well with us: we like your flat more every day: have all our meals on the terrace, when the wind isn't too strong. I find it lovely and cool and am writing a story about Venice. Later I want to write one about Florence: modern, of course... Peggy is pretty well, I think. She's not going to die of a broken heart, whatever else she dies of. So don't flatter yourself. Yesterday Tina gave her a bath on the terrace here, in the red trough. She trembled and looked pathetic, but loved all the notice taken of her. Poor Tina has trouble with her teeth, bad inflammation of the lower gums: looks a wretch and feels it.' The editor of Lawrence's letters, Harry T. Moore, helpfully points out that 'Tina was probably Nelly Morrison's maid, and Peggy a dog.'

Mentally Lawrence was very robust, and he tended to be harsh on the less robust: of E.M. Forster he wrote 'his life is ridiculously inane, the man is dying of inanition.' After Lawrence himself died of tuberculosis in the south of France in 1931, his letters were edited by Aldous Huxley. (Forster, by the way, lived to be over ninety.)

The architect and landscape garden designer CECIL PINSENT (1884-1963) came to Florence in 1907, and together with GEOFFREY SCOTT (1884-1929) he became part of the Berenson circle. Mary Berenson got rid of her Italian architects and took on Pinsent and Scott to restore the house and gardens at I Tatti. Pinsent had worked in an architect's office and had a certain amount of technical expertise, whereas the approach of his lazy business partner Geoffrey Scott was purely aesthetic and historical. (Scott did however write a good book on *The Architecture of Humanism*, which is still in print after more than a century.) In the spring of 1909, Pinsent and Scott, 'with lists as long as their long legs', set to work at I

Geoffrey Scott and Cecil Pinsent

Tatti, wiring the villa, whitewashing the walls and restoring all the floors, while Bernard and Mary took up temporary quarters in nearby Villa Linda. Mary, who referred to the pair as her 'artichokes', tried to persuade Scott to become a proper architect, and he accordingly enrolled in the Architecture Association's School in London, but his name appears on the rolls for that term only. Finding the discipline of applied study and measured drawing far too boring, he soon abandoned it and became a sort of aesthetic theorist, helping Pinsent in an advisory capacity, choosing furnishings and fittings for their various clients. Pinsent sometimes exasperated Mary: 'Today I have been grappling with Cecil, who just slides through one's fingers like an eel. He never finishes anything, and BB is getting crazy with these months of temporary makeshifts.' Eventually, in 1910, Pinsent and Scott did form a partnership, taking rooms in Florence in via delle Terme, to serve as studio and living quarters. There was a wonderful view of the Duomo from their windows. While the flat was being prepared, Scott lived at I Tatti, to Mary's great delight. On 11 March 1911 Pinsent wrote to Mary: 'The garden is going merrily and really is going to look well. All the muratore work is about half done—laghetti, steps, paving, & the planting of the rustic wall. We are getting quite excited about it. The avenue now that it has been tidied, and the lines straightened, looks genuinely successful; and makes one feel that the garden will not be a failure after all.' As for the Library, on 13 August he told Mary that he would be staying around at I Tatti 'so as to be able to have more time to contrive the mechanism of the Library secret door; as you can imagine this is going to give me more fun than anything else.' Throughout the previous year, Pinsent had continued working for Charles Loeser, planning a loggia, and he also produced designs for the Duveen Gallery at Place Vendôme, Paris.

EDITH SITWELL (1887-1964), the eldest of the three arty siblings whose father had bought the large and crumbling castle of Montegufoni not far from Florence, visited the city fairly often. Her enormous jewellery and elaborate coiffures astonished the Florentines. On one occasion in January 1957 she lectured at the British Institute on 'Modern British Poetry'. No doubt she read her famous wartime poem 'Still falls the rain', in her customary incantatory fashion. Afterwards there occurred an incident whose moral seems to be 'Don't mess with a Sitwell'. As she described in a letter: 'On galloped an enormous young man, and sucking down my hand like a swamp in Florida and gluing his face to mine, he enquired "Do you know who I am?" I said coldly that I didn't. Whereupon he said some name that I had never heard of, Hannikin or Hennikin, and said "My father told me to ask you if you remember sitting on his knee"!!!! There was a deathly silence. I drew myself up and absolutely glared at him... The young man added as an afterthought "As a child". I said "I never sat on anybody's knee as a child and I have never heard of your father", and turned my back. But it was a nine days' wonder in Florence.' Assuredly, Dame Edith had a high sense of her own dignity.

The soldier, spy and translator CHARLES KENNETH SCOTT MONCRIEFF (1889-1930) first came to Florence for his health in October 1923. In the previous year he had published the first volume of his magisterial translation of Marcel Proust's *À la recherche du temps perdu*, to which he gave the Shakespearean title *Remembrance of Things Past*. As a soldier in the Great War he had converted to Catholicism. In Florence he and his parents, George and Meg, stayed at the Hotel Balestri in piazza Mentana, where D.H. Lawrence and Norman Douglas had stayed before them. Their bedroom windows overlooked the Arno. There Charles continued with his translation, completing the first volume of *Le Côté de Guermantes*, and sent it to his publishers by diplomatic bag. Being a translator was a good cover for intelligence activities, as he was able to travel freely, and he did a certain amount of spying on the Fascist regime, for H.M. Government. Scott Moncrieff made friends with Norman Douglas, who lived just round the corner from the Balestri on lungarno delle Grazie, and with Reggie Turner, whose flat was at 35 viale Giovanni Milton. 'Old queens bickering round a teapot,' was how D.H. Lawrence described

Edith Sitwell

Charles Kenneth Scott Moncrieff

Charles and Reggie. Charles received many visits from Vyvyan Holland, Oscar Wilde's son, with whom he exchanged gay banter. On 23 December 1923 he and his parents were still at the Balestri, where he developed 'a sort of Proust reading circle among the guests.' Shortly after this the three of them moved to Rapallo on the riviera, where Reggie Turner came from Florence to visit Charles and introduced him to Max Beerbohm. Max and his wife Florence lived in Rapallo. Rather tactlessly, he told Charles that he did not like Proust and never had.

After a while Scott Moncrieff returned to Florence and moved into a house on the steep costa San Giorgio, on the south side of the river. It was owned by the painter Stephen Haweis, who had been married to Mina Loy, the Bohemian artist, novelist and lamp designer. The house was noisy, and Charles suspected there might have been some sort of sawmill on the roof, 'but it is all very jolly, and when warmer weather comes, I shall be able to work on the roof, which commands a boundless view of Florence across the river.' Also living in this house were 'a number of drug addicts' and another artist, the Johannesburg-born Edward Wolfe, who took Charles to visit Bernard Berenson at I Tatti. Charles found it difficult to concentrate on his work while in Florence, for apart from the noise there was a steady stream of visitors from Britain—friends of friends—who expected him to show them round the galleries and churches. So he moved to a very primitive village near Lucca, Cerasomma, where he took a break from Proust and started translating Stendhal, the letters of Héloïse and Abélard, and Pirandello. Of the latter, Charles wrote to Vyvyan: 'I am going to translate the complete works of Pirandello, in two hundred and eighteen volumes; it will be very difficult, as I do not know any Italian.'

In Pisa in the spring of 1927 Scott Moncrieff wrote that he was 'being harassed by a dreary attempt at blackmail', though whether this was to do with espionage or sex is not clear. He decided to leave Pisa and 'offer the bulk of my library to the British Institute in Florence. What a woundily long book Proust is. I met D.H. Lawrence yesterday [3 May] for the first time. An odd spectacle: also his German wife. I must go out now and take a bath with some verbena salts, spoils of Florence, which may ôter le cafard, but I doubt it.' Like Reggie Turner, Charles thought Lawrence's *Lady Chatterley's Lover* 'indescribably filthy'. Filthiness is a subjective matter, and indeed Lawrence wrote to Richard Aldington: 'Scott Moncrieff said he'd write to you. He has a nice side to him—but really an obscene mind like a lavatory.'

Lawrence did in fact enjoy Charles's witty conversation, and late in 1929 he wrote to Pino Orioli: 'Poor Scott Moncrieff, I hope it's not cancer.' It was, of the stomach. On his deathbed in Rome, Charles was visited by G.K. Chesterton, who read Virgil to him in Latin, and by Evelyn Waugh, who gave him 'the first blissful evening I've had for months'. He died on 28 February 1930, two days before Lawrence.

The English poet, critic, novelist and biographer RICHARD ALDINGTON (1892-1962) visited Villa La Pietra in January 1931. On that occasion he was accompanied by his mistress Brigit Patmore, whose daughter-in-law he later married. A fortnight before Aldington's visit, an article by him had appeared in the *Sunday Referee*, discussing Harold Acton's translation of an anonymous eighteenth-century memoir, and its impending prosecution for indecency. The translation had been published in Florence in a limited edition as no. 2 of the 'Lungarno Series', with an introduction by Norman Douglas, and was entitled *The Last of the Medici*. (It should not be confused with Harold's *The Last Medici*.) Fortunately, the case came up before a sensible judge who dismissed it. Richard and Brigit seem to

Aldous Huxley

Richard Aldington

have got on well with Harold and Norman, and the four of them lunched and dined several times together, in trattorias such as Bettis, where they devoured 'macaroni & white truffles, ducklings from the Maremma, Dutch cheese.' Norman never visited La Pietra, on principle, but Richard and Brigit no doubt enjoyed themselves, taking tea with Harold's parents.

Richard had first visited Florence in December 1912 on his way to meet the American poet Hilda Dolittle, known as 'H.D.', whom he was to marry in 1913. Having published his war novel *Death of a Hero* in 1929, he returned to Florence in late 1930 or early 1931, this time with Brigid, having long been separated from H.D. They had come to Florence partly to meet Norman Douglas, and they stayed at the Gran Bretagna Hotel overlooking the Arno. Douglas was away when they arrived, and in the meanwhile they were entertained by Pino Orioli, whom Richard had known at Orioli's London bookshop before the Great War. In November 1931 they returned for a six-month stay, renting a flat at piazza Santa Croce no. 12 and frequently lunching with Norman Douglas. Richard would later recall his memories of Douglas and Orioli in his memoir *Pinorman*, published in 1954.

The Surrey-born essayist and novelist ALDOUS HUXLEY (1894-1963), who had poor eyesight and looked like a willowy giraffe, came to Florence with his young Belgian wife Maria in March 1921. They had a baby son called Matthew, and they settled into a wing of the Villa Minucci, in via Santa Maria Montici, close to Castel Montici. On 1 April Aldous wrote to his father Leonard: 'The flat is furnished adequately though somewhat hideously and we pay a hundred and fifty lire [about £18] a month for it, which is not much... From the western windows we get a marvellous view—a valley sloping away from the house in the foreground, planted with olives and vines, with the church of San Miniato on the hill on the opposite side; to the right, looking down the valley, we see almost the whole of Florence lying in the plain, a sort of Oxford from Boar's Hill effect, only very much more so.'

Aldous had known D.H. Lawrence during the War at Garsington, the home of Lady Ottoline Morrell, and now in Florence they became intimate friends. Huxley noted in his diary: 'Lunched and spent the p.m. with the Lawrences. DHL in admirable form, talking wonderfully. He is one of the few people I feel real respect and admiration for.' *Crome Yellow*, a satire on the Garsington set, was published in 1921: Lady Ottoline never forgave Aldous for its caricature of her. The Huxleys returned to Florence for a month in 1923, this time at the Castel Montici itself, and there Aldous wrote *Antic Hay*, which appeared later that year. He complained about the discomforts: the electric pump failed, and all the water had to be carried in buckets to the kitchen and bathrooms; the architecture was ugly; recent decoration had been shoddily carried out. But again there was the compensation of a 'marvellous position', with breath-taking views over Florence and up the Arno valley as far as the Apennines. Huxley's short story 'Young Archimedes' has a lyrical description of the view towards Florence: '...looking over the low dark shoulder of the hill on whose extreme promontory stood the towered church of San Miniato, one saw the huge dome airily hanging on its ribs of masonry, the square campanile, the sharp spire of Santa Croce, and the canopied tower of the Signoria, rising above the intricate maze of the houses, distinct and brilliant, like small treasures carved out of precious stones.' In a letter to his father, Aldous said Florence was packed with English visitors, but that he and Maria seldom ventured into town to see them. Among those they did see were Vernon Lee, John Mavrogordato, Norman Douglas and Geoffrey Scott.

Vernon Lee was living at the Villa Palmerino. Mavrogordato achieved fame as the English translator of the Greek poet Constantine Cavafy, whose great promoter and champion in England was E.M. Forster. Norman Douglas was at this time staying at no. 24 via de' Benci. He really hated most of the things that people love about Florence. Geoffrey Scott was the very lazy business partner of the hardworking landscape architect Cecil Pinsent; he was married to Lady Sybil Cutting, the mother of Iris Origo.

Huxley may have liked these four people, but in general he regarded the English colony as 'a sort of decayed provincial intelligentsia'. At that time it would have included the novelist and biographer Richard Aldington, and the translator C.K. Scott Moncrieff. Huxley was no doubt overreacting to the praise heaped on Florence by nineteenth-century visitors when he wrote: 'The spectacle of that second-rate provincial town with its repulsive Gothic architecture and its acres of Christmas-card primitives made me almost sick.' It is evident that he felt himself to be somewhat superior to the Anglo-Florentines. In *Along the Road* (1925) he wrote: 'Florence is the home of those who cultivate with an equal ardour Mah-jongg and a passion for Fra Angelico. Over tea and crumpets they talk, if they are too old for love themselves, of their lascivious juniors; but they also make sketches in water colour and read the Little Flowers of St Francis.'

Like C.S. Lewis, Aldous Huxley died on the day that President Kennedy was assassinated.

The Yorkshire sculptor HENRY MOORE (1898-1982) first came to Italy on a five-month travelling scholarship in 1925. He spent three of the five months in Florence, being (as he wrote in a letter in 1972) at 'the most impressionable stage' of his artistic development. At first he studied the early Florentine masters, especially Giotto, whom he admired 'for his evident sculptural qualities.' Later he became obsessed with Masaccio, and early each morning would hurry to the Brancacci Chapel in the church of the Carmine, to study the marvellous frescoes of the *Tribute Money*, *St Peter Curing the Cripples with his Shadow*, *Adam and Eve Expelled from Paradise*, *The Baptism of the Neophytes* and *The Distribution of Alms and the Death of Ananias*. Towards the end of his three months it was Michelangelo who most attracted him, and he was to remain enchanted by the great Tuscan master for the rest of his life.

In the mid-1960s Moore bought a house at Forte de' Marmi, at the foot of the Apuan Alps, and he and his family would spend two months there each year, while he worked on his marble sculptures. 'When I need refreshing in spirit, in little over an hour from our house I can be in Florence surrounded by the great paintings and sculptures I love', he said.

Forty-seven years after his first visit, Moore had achieved an international reputation, with monumental sculptures in public locations all over the world. The crowning of his career was the major retrospective exhibition held in 1972 at the Forte Belvedere overlooking Florence. On 15 May Moore and his wife Irina lunched at La Pietra with Harold Acton. Three days later Princess Margaret and her husband Lord Snowden came to stay with Harold: she visited the British Institute on the morning of the 20th, and in the afternoon she opened the Moore exhibition. The weather was bitterly cold, but the exhibition was judged a huge success. Indeed, in Moore's opinion, 'No better site for showing sculpture in the open-air, in relation to architecture and to a town, could be found anywhere in the world than the Forte di Belvedere with its impressive environs and its wonderful panoramic views of the city.' In recent times, Antony Gormley has exhibited his sculptures at the Forte. Moore wrote a number of books about his own sculpture and drawings.

In 1928, H.V.F. SOMERSET (1898-1965) published a slim volume called *Half a Hundred Epigrams*. One of the short poems is about the Ponte Vecchio, and another is entitled 'On the city of Florence':

> 'God made the country, and man made the town'—
> Wise words, first heard by me, long since, at school!
> Yet this corollary I too must own—
> 'Florence the exception is that proves the rule.'

(In order not to be involved in a logical absurdity, we must here take 'proves' as meaning 'tests the limits of'.)

On 9 May 1938 Benito Mussolini scrawled *'Firenze fascistissima!!'* in the visitors' book at Palazzo Vecchio. He was delighted by his and Adolf Hitler's reception in the city. As the War was about to break out, numerous foreigners left Florence, and then many of those who did not were interned. From 1943 to 1944 the city was under German occupation. On 25 September 1943 the Allies bombed central Florence, killing 215 civilians and destroying many buildings. The beautiful Ponte Santa Trìnita was blown to smithereens by the retreating Wehrmacht, together with four other bridges, in early August 1944. On the 11th, the English newspapers reported 'All Florence in Allied Hands'.

The conservative Catholic novelist EVELYN WAUGH (1903-1966) paid three visits to Harold Acton in Italy in the 1950s and 1960s. I should like to focus on a literary dinner party, a 'social and culinary failure', that took place in Florence in April 1950, during the first of Waugh's three visits. In the spring of that year Harold's amusing novella *Prince Isidore* had just been published. Evelyn, whom Harold had not seen since the War, wrote out of the blue praising the novella ('What a delight Prince Isidore is!') and inviting himself to stay.

Evelyn Waugh

Waugh spent Holy Week in Rome, where he heard Mass sung in San Pietro by Pope Pius XII Pacelli, then came up to Florence to meet Harold. They dined together at the Villa Natalia on the La Pietra estate, which was a pensione in those days. On the following day Harold took Evelyn to San Lorenzo and to the Bargello, and they dined in the restaurant Olivero in via delle Terme; it was there that Sinclair Lewis—as Harold recalled in his memoirs—'loped diagonally across the room to our table and hailed him [Waugh] as a dear old pal. Evelyn looked startled...'. This inauspicious beginning resulted in the painful dinner party described on pp. 307-309 of Acton's *More Memoirs of an Aesthete*. 'Red' Lewis, author of *Main Street* and *Babbitt*, had in 1930 become the first American to win the Nobel Prize in Literature. At this time his health was not at all good, in fact he was to die in Rome the following year, 1951; he was trying to finish a book, was drinking a good deal, and was living in a kitsch rented house on pian dei Giullari, Villa La Costa. Red told Harold and Evelyn that he had not given a dinner party for months, but was most pressing that they should both come.

Evelyn had by this date completely shed the fun-loving, party-going persona that had entranced Harold in the iconoclastic 1920s; in its place he had fully assumed the cantankerous, reactionary persona of his later years. His country house in Gloucestershire, Piers Court, where he lived with his wife Laura and their six children, had a sign outside that read 'No admittance on business'. When abroad he refused to speak any language but English, which he expected everyone to understand, and he was consistently rude to waiters and to anyone else who annoyed him. One example of his appalling rudeness will be more than sufficient. A friendly American told him how much she had enjoyed his novel *Brideshead Revisited*, whereupon he rolled his eyes and replied: 'I thought it was good myself, but now I know that a vulgar, common American woman like you admires it, I'm not so sure.' (This makes him sound odious, of course; but he was much loved by a large circle of friends, and he was often spontaneously generous. In a televised interview after his death, Nancy Mitford said: 'What nobody remembers about Evelyn is that everything with him was jokes. Everything. That's what none of the people who wrote about him seem to have taken into account.')

Anyway, Harold Acton thought that in the whole of Florence Lewis could not have chosen a more hideous, garish house in which to live. Harold found the ugliness of the rooms, furniture and pictures quite depressing, no doubt comparing them in his mind with the splendours of La Pietra. Evelyn visited Osbert Sitwell at Montegufoni, but was back in Florence in good time for Lewis's dinner party.

Also invited together with Harold and Evelyn were Una Lady Troubridge, who for twenty-eight years had been the companion of Radclyffe Hall, the monocle-wearing, dog-loving authoress of the celebrated Lesbian novel *The Well of Loneliness* (which Lewis had defended when it was banned in the late 1920s); Red's half-Polish secretary, Alec

Manson; and Manson's Florentine girlfriend, Tina Lazzerini. Lewis had apparently been eating little and drinking plenty—when he wrote he could scarcely bring himself to eat and he was just on the verge of finishing a novel about modern Florence—and consequently his speech was incoherent and obscure. They were offered tiny glasses of weak vermouth and a poor dinner of tepid spaghetti, veal and sweet whipped cream cake with watered wine—watered by the secretary because Lewis was apt to drink too much of it! These horrid catering arrangements evidently did not improve the mood of the guests. Their host did not touch his food and burped loudly and long several times during dinner.

Evelyn's face was a study, as he flinched and sat back in his chair. Some of the halting and awkward conversation is reproduced in Harold's *More Memoirs of an Aesthete*, published in 1970. 'Evelyn flinched in his chair on the host's right with an expression of growing alarm. "What is that frightful noise?", he kept asking me. Red's speech was incoherent but at length he noticed that Evelyn was fasting and he urged him to taste the veal, the *spécialité de la maison*. Evelyn answered severely: "It's Friday". Diverted by this, Red prompted his companion, who had been an army captain serving in Trieste, to entertain us with the saga of his war exploits. "I don't want to hear them", said Evelyn. "Oh but you must. They're absolutely hilarious. Tell Evelyn about the holy-water font that was mistaken for a urinal". The captain, an ingenuous type, proceeded to spin his yarns, which convulsed Red with guffaws interspersed with hiccups. Evelyn pressed his fingers to his ears and sat back with an air of weary resignation. Towards the climax he turned to me and asked: "Has he finished?" When I nodded he removed his fingers and contemplated the table cloth. Lady Troubridge strove to remedy the gaffe, but the dinner was a social and culinary failure.'

After dinner they were taken on a tour the house—Lewis seemed quite aware of its hideousness but rather pleased and amused by it at the same time—and they sat in his bedroom beside the fire while he maundered on about how much he had enjoyed writing his novel—'it may be bad, but it has given me a lot of fun', he kept repeating.

The novel Lewis was working on was called *World so Wide*, his twenty-second, and it was published posthumously in 1951.

According to Harold's memoirs, Red Lewis was provoked by what he took to be Evelyn Waugh's standoffishness, and 'delivered a panegyric upon the vigour, the splendour, the creative genius of America, which was moving in the circumstances despite its platitudes... Red's bloodshot eyes bulged, his fingers trembled clutching the chair, as he wound up with a denunciation of contemporary English literature... Evelyn reddened more with embarrassment than resentment, but he endured it all most patiently and politely. I suspect he was aware of the pathos underlying this... defiant monologue. "I can't think what got into him," said Lady Troubridge when we escorted her home. "I'm afraid poor old Red is off colour. He doesn't usually behave like that, I assure you." "I rather enjoyed the latter part of it", said Evelyn. "I was only afraid he might burst a blood vessel".'

From Paris Evelyn sent a postcard, sending his love to 'Red Lewis, Mrs Walston and all stray yanks' (Catherine Walston was Graham Greene's American mistress, and they had been staying at the Villa Natalia; by 'yanks' he means Americans in general, not necessarily ones from New England). In a letter to Evelyn later that year, Harold thanked him for the copy of his novel *Helena*, and reported that Red Lewis seemed to have departed, but that Una Troubridge still plodded via Tornabuoni, 'hatless and grim'. And that phrase is the final ripple from the unsuccessful dinner party at Villa La Costa, so far as I have been able to discover.

The art historian and museum director KENNETH CLARK (1903-1983) first came to Florence in the summer of 1925, having just completed his history degree at Trinity College, Oxford. He travelled with his much older friend Charlie Bell, director of the Ashmolean Museum, and they stayed at Poggio Gherardo with fierce old Janet Ross. Not far from Mrs Ross's house was the Berensons' Villa I Tatti, and it was at a luncheon there that Berenson impulsively offered to take Kenneth on as his assistant, so that they could work together on a new edition of *Drawings of the Florentine Painters*, first published in the year of Kenneth's birth. The twenty-two-year-old Englishman later spoke of his debt to Berenson as 'difficult to describe and impossible to repay.' In January 1926 he spent a couple of weeks in the Library at I Tatti, and in November that year he settled down to work there.

Many years later, after a successful career as Director of the National Gallery, Kenneth and his wife Jane returned to war-damaged Florence in the spring of 1947. Of this visit he wrote to Berenson: 'You can hardly imagine what an impression Italy makes after eight years in this island— and especially after the squalor and misery of the last winter. The eye has become so starved, and there seems no possibility of new life. Everything is either filthy or crumbling, or bleak and thread bare to the last degree. The sight of the olive trees and blossom in the country, and of the vigorous, confident architecture of the town [Florence], was more impressive, at this moment, than any individual works of art.'

In his 1956 classic *The Nude*, Sir Kenneth wrote: 'The Venus of Giorgione is sleeping, without a thought of her nakedness. Compared with Titian's Venus of Urbino, she is like a bud, wrapped in its sheath, each petal folded so firmly as to give us the feeling of inflexible purpose. With Titian, the bud has opened.'

In his celebrated 1969 television series *Civilisation*, Lord Clark—as he had by then become—spoke most eloquently about the greatness of Florence in the early Renaissance: 'There is no better instance of how a burst of civilisation depends on confidence, than the Florentine state of mind in the early fifteenth century.' Having shown on the screen the majestic heads of the Apostles from Masaccio's *The Tribute Money*, he concluded: 'The Florentine republic… was directed by a group of the most intelligent individuals who have ever been elected to power by a democratic government. The Florentine chancellors were scholars, believers in the *studia humanitatis*, in which learning could be used to achieve a happy life, believers in the application of free intelligence to public affairs, believers—above all—in Florence.'

HAROLD ACTON (1904-1994) was not a visitor because, like Frederick Stibbert, he was born in Florence (not far from where Stibbert lived). He was however the *doyen* of the Anglo-Florentine community, as well as being a versatile writer in several genres: poetry, history, novels and novellas, short stories, translations from the Chinese, biography and autobiography. Born at his parents' villa on via Bolognese, he enjoyed a privileged and cosmopolitan childhood. The 'residential colony' in Florence at this time included many occupants of villas in the surrounding hills: they all visited each other's houses, spending many hours of each day gossiping. Arthur, descended from the Italian branch of the Acton

Kenneth Clark

Harold Acton

family, and his wife Hortense, an heiress from Chicago, had moved into Villa La Pietra on their marriage in 1903. Princess Ghyka and Florence Blood lived together at the Villa Gamberaia, where the gardens were so much admired by Arthur, and they would invite Harold and his brother William to visit them, when there were children of their own age. In the summer of 1910 there was an elegant wedding at La Pietra, when Harold's cousin Louise Gaylord married Walter Dillingham of Hawaii: Harold and William were pages, and were photographed outside the Villa with such wedding guests as 'Mrs Gerritt Wilder, Governor and Mrs George Carter, and Chicago's famous art collectors, Mr and Mrs Potter Palmer', in their cartwheel hats and Edwardian gowns.

At the age of six Harold attended Miss Penrose's school for boys and girls, apparently at the Villa Lalleta. He then studied French with Mlle Marie Horny, 'an old crone with parchment cheeks and coal-black eyes', in via Madonna della Tosse. Around this time Harold drew some charming and imaginative pictures of princesses, orientals and witches.

He was sent away to prep school at Wixenford in England, where he was very miserable, and then after the outbreak of the Great War, to the international school at Château Lancy in Geneva. There he perfected his French. After a short time in a dreadful 'crammer' he went to Eton, and thence to Christ Church, Oxford.

From all these establishments he was always delighted to return

La Pietra

home in the holidays to La Pietra, where his conversational skills in English, French and Italian were improved by contact with his parents' sophisticated circle of international acquaintances. He had several visitors from England. One year during the Easter holidays his old schoolfellow Robert Byron, who was travelling round Europe with the family of Lord Beauchamp (the original of Lord Marchmain in *Brideshead Revisited*), lunched with Harold and his parents at La Pietra. Robert found the house the loveliest he had ever seen, 'filled with priceless pictures, stuffs, bits of carving, statues, marvellous plate.' Harold took Robert to his favourite Florentine haunts: Doney's, the 'tearoom where more whisky is consumed than tea', and the nightclub Raiola's. Both at Eton and at Christ Church Harold appeared very much older and more assured than his contemporaries. Indeed he was by far the most prominent and flamboyant undergraduate of his generation, though his academic career was undistinguished. At Oxford he wrote poetry, and his first book *Aquarium* (1923) was widely reviewed in the national press. His real literary talent was however for historical prose, and in May 1932 his *The Last Medici* was published by Faber & Faber. Covering the reigns of the Grand Dukes Cosimo III and Gian Gastone, it is a narrative *tour de force*, an exploration of a period that was totally unfamiliar to English readers at the time, and a genuine literary triumph for its twenty-seven-year-old author. By that time he had set off for China, where he was to remain for seven years, teaching English literature at the Pei Ta National University in Peking and studying the classical Chinese theatre. Late in 1936 he decided to return to Europe for a short visit: on 28 November he sailed from Shanghai on the *Conte Rosso*, intending to disembark either at Venice or at Bari and to arrive at La Pietra in time for Christmas Day.

'The city of Florence never changes, but on the surface it had grown more garish, owing to the influx of bright uniforms', Harold recalled of his return to his native city. He found militaristic slogans scrawled on the walls, and a shockingly anti-British feeling in the air. But he revelled in the wonderful view from Norman Douglas's flat on the lungarno delle Grazie, looking south-east towards San Miniato as the sun went down, and he realised that Florence had never lost its hold over him. Contessa Rucellai called Harold her *cher chinois*, and he enjoyed seeing Reggie Turner and other old friends, but it seems that there was little to detain him at La Pietra and by 10 February 1937 he was in Paris, on his way back to Peking. He returned to Europe in 1939, after his beloved China had been invaded by the Japanese.

Early in the Second World War, before Mussolini had declared war on Britain, Harold made a quixotic lecture tour of Italy to try and persuade the Italians that they were Britain's friends. He gave his first lecture in a 'disappointingly small room' at the British Institute in Milan, and after repeating his talk in Genoa he arrived in Florence on 5 March. His parents had not seen him for nearly three years, but they were not at all pleased about this lecture tour of his: Arthur and Hortense Acton made it all too obvious that they feared Harold 'would make a fool of [him]self and put them to shame.' However, the talk he gave at the British Institute in Florence seems to have been a great success: the director Francis Toye was there, as well as his two predecessors Arthur Spender and Harold Goad. It was his courageous lecture tour that earned Harold the affection of the Jewish and anti-Fascist Bernard Berenson.

Harold did his wartime service in the Royal Air Force, mostly in India and Ceylon, where he had various desk jobs. After the liberation of Paris he went there as an intelligence officer, and delighted in the company of old Parisian friends such as Cocteau, Picasso and Gertrude

Stein. In the summer of 1945 he was posted to occupied Germany, and at Minden he learned of the lonely death of his brother William, a victim of alcoholism and substance-abuse. From Minden Harold proceeded to England where at Uxbridge he was at last demobilised, and immediately set out on the tortuous journey across war-ravaged France by train. At Bologna he was given a lift by lorry to Florence: 'dusty and exhausted', he trudged up the cypress-lined drive to the Villa, its façade glowing golden in the evening sun. He found his mother prostrated with grief, his father hostile. Both parents made it painfully obvious to Harold that they would have preferred to lose their elder rather than their younger son. Arthur Acton appeared to indicate that he held Harold personally responsible for William's demise.

Nevertheless, Harold decided to live with his parents in Florence. James Lees-Milne noted about Arthur and Hortense Acton: 'They nag Harold and ask him to fetch ash-trays, to ring the bell, to turn on and off lights and generally fag. All this he does with good humour as a matter of course.' He was now in his forties, but according to his friend James Lord he still did not have a key to La Pietra, and if he stayed out late he had to climb in through a window. Lord was not impressed by Arthur Acton ('an unattractive, peevish individual, speaking very little and scowling at the guests'), who he said used to closet himself away from the rest of the household and sip champagne with shady antique dealers. About William's death, James Lord wrote to me: 'I suspect his feeling for his brother was somewhat tainted by the fact that William was handsome and the favored son' [18 December 2004].

Partly to get away from his parents, and partly to research his historical books on the Bourbons, Harold moved in 1950 to Naples where he took a flat at via Posillipo no. 37. His life settled into a routine, moving between his new flat and La Pietra. Arthur died in March 1953, and Harold reorganised the library, something he had evidently been forbidden to do while his father was alive. About Arthur's death, Violet Trefusis wrote that he was so representative of Florence that it was as though Doney's had disappeared in the night. Harold and his mother began to think about what to do with La Pietra.

That summer he visited Ischia, where 'Auden and his gang' were in evidence, and spent more time in Naples. On his visits to his mother in Florence he enjoyed seeing Osbert Sitwell and his friend David Horner at the castle of Montegufoni, and also the Revd Victor Stanley, the sociable American Episcopalian clergyman who was such an amusing conversationalist. Early in 1954 Harold travelled to London, where he worked on the English sources of his Neapolitan history in the British Museum and the Public Record Office. It was while he was in London that James Lord wrote to him, posing the crucial question: 'What has La Pietra given you compared with what it has taken away?'; this was a question Harold was able to answer neither then nor at any other time.

In 1956 Methuen published Harold's *The Bourbons of Naples (1734-1825)*, which five years later was followed by *The Last Bourbons of Naples (1825-1861)*. These two volumes may be said to constitute Harold's masterpiece, a detailed, enthralling and gripping exercise in the unfashionable genre of narrative history.

His American mother Hortense died in November 1962, and letters of condolence poured in. The depressive English writer T.H. White came to stay, and his somewhat odd company may have been exactly what Harold needed. To the painter Derek Hill he wrote 'I always adored my mother and I miss her more and more.'

Now that both of his parents were dead and he was at last the sole owner of La Pietra, Harold could have done anything he wanted. James Lord believed that Harold should have got rid of the Villa, which with its 3,000 works of art had become an oppressive burden. At last he was free of the tedious round of tea parties and drinks parties that his parents had instituted. So what did he do? He continued in exactly the same fashion for the next thirty years.

His work on behalf of the British Institute, together with his friendship with the royal family—Princess Margaret came to stay at La Pietra on several occasions—led to his knighthood in 1974.

Harold Acton wrote a number of books with Florentine or Tuscan themes. *Florence*, illustrated by the photographer Martin Hürlimann, had appeared in 1960. It was followed by *Tuscan Villas* in 1973, *The Pazzi Conspiracy* in 1979, *The Soul's Gymnasium* (a collection of short stories set in Florence) in 1982 and *Florence: a Traveller's Companion*, written with his friend Edward Chaney in 1986 (new edition 2018). Taken together, these books provide a unique overview of the city by one who knew it and loved it well through a long and varied life.

Graham Greene

Nancy Mitford

In the 1950s the left-wing Catholic novelist GRAHAM GREENE (1904-1991) came several times to Florence to visit Harold Acton, who had been his contemporary at Oxford, where they had a somewhat prickly relationship: Harold slagged off Graham's poetry in the undergraduate magazine the *Cherwell*. Writing years later to his fiancée, Graham recalled '... the person I miss now... is Harold. It was such intense fun, our mutual "hate". And I do respect him. Although I wouldn't admit it to anyone else, his attack in the Cherwell was the best & most awful criticism I've ever had, & my alterations I try to make to my stuff are founded on it.' And much later he wrote to Evelyn Waugh: 'In Italy we saw Harold. How nice & dear he is, & how I didn't realise it at Oxford.' Graham remarks somewhere that Evelyn would chide him on his single-minded heterosexuality, and would tell him that a homosexual phase was a desirable attribute for a novelist, but he would not be persuaded. Graham came several times to La Pietra, and several times he stayed at the pensione in nearby Villa Natalia, accompanied by his beautiful American mistress Catherine Walston (and on one occasion also by her mother). One evening the pair of them sent Harold a note to La Pietra, a heart with an arrow through it drawn on Villa Natalia writing paper, and an invitation to come and drink whisky with them. I do not know, but I imagine he accepted with alacrity: they sound to have been having such fun.

The novelist and biographer NANCY MITFORD (1904-1973) was one of the six celebrated Mitford sisters, whose political allegiances were extremely varied. She was great friends with Evelyn Waugh and Harold Acton (her exact contemporary), and wrote a string of amusing novels. During the War she worked in Heywood Hill's bookshop in Curzon Street, where customers who were quick on the uptake were greeted with 'radiant smiles', and dull ones were 'given hell'. In 1965 she came to Florence to stay with her old friend at Villa La Pietra, from 13 to 21 September. She enjoyed herself very much. On the 25th she wrote to Heywood Hill: 'I've been staying with Harold—perfect heaven, everything I like best. One wakes up in a room longer than the Chatsworth drawing room [in the home of her youngest sister, the Duchess of Devonshire, who had always wanted to marry 'the Duke of Right'] with sun streaming onto the bed... Then the art, both in the house & in the galleries, knocked me silly. We lunched & dined out in wonderful villas—with such gardens.' After her death from cancer in 1973, Acton wrote a charming memoir of her, in which he carefully avoided naming Nancy's long-term lover ('The Colonel'). As soon as the book came out, all the reviewers took delight in identifying the 'Colonel' as the French politician Gaston Palewski (1901-1984).

In the summer of 1947 the boozy Welsh poet DYLAN THOMAS (1914-1953) came to Florence because he and his family had been lent the Villa Beccaro at Mosciano near Scandicci. He wrote to his parents: 'It's on the hills, above Florence, some five miles or more from the centre, from the great Cathedral dome which we can see from the sunbathing terrace above the swimming pool. And I hope that sounds grand enough. It's a very big villa with huge rooms and lovely grounds, arbours, terraces, pools... There are cypresses and palms all around us, in the wide green valley below with poppies among the vines and olives... Nightingales sing all night long. Lizards scuttle out of the walls in the sun.' In another letter he said he and his wife Caitlin were living on asparagus, artichokes, gorgonzola, strawberries, olive oil and lots of red wine. To Donald Taylor he wrote: 'The heat is sizzling, the wine overpowering, the villa enormous.' Despite these idyllic surroundings Dylan was not really happy in Tuscany and he took a dim view of the local Florentine intellectuals. 'I like the people I don't know in the streets, but not the writers, etc., who are nearly all editors, I meet in the cafés. So many of them live with their mothers, on private incomes, and translate Apollinaire... [Eugenio] Montale seems to be an exception', he wrote to Ronald Bottrall, and to John Davenport he explained: '[The local writers] visit us on Sunday. To overcome the language, I have to stand on my head, fall into the swimming pool, crack nuts with my teeth, and Tarzan in the cypresses.' The poet Mario Luzi, who was also born in 1914, was somewhat bewildered by Dylan's constant heavy drinking. 'Entering the Giubbe Rosse [the literary café in piazza della Repubblica] late of an evening, he was to be found entrenched behind a small forest of bottles, a full glass

Dylan Thomas

in his hand, and one wondered whether those large pale blue eyes were gazing on something ineffable or merely into vacancy. He would begin to speak, then lapse into silence, perhaps because the listener did not understand English, perhaps because what he had to say was inexpressible in any language.' Dylan's biographer Constantine FitzGibbon, himself a great drinker, comments on this passage: 'If this is a good example of the writing of the Florentine intellectuals, and if many of them were so unobservant as to think that Dylan had blue eyes, his somnolence becomes more than excusable.' His eyes were green. FitzGibbon, by the bye, was a nephew of Norman Douglas's wife Elsa. By mid-July Dylan was writing to his friend Tommy Earp: 'I am awfully sick of it here, on the beautiful hills above Florence, drinking Chianti in our marble shanty, sick of vini and contadini and bambini, and sicker still when I go, bumpy with mosquito bites, into Florence itself, which is a gruelling museum.' As Dylan Thomas made so little effort to integrate, it serves him right that he got so little from his Florentine experience. It was the only period he ever spent abroad, until the American tours that ended with his fatal trip to New York in 1953. His last words were: 'I've had eighteen straight whiskies, I think that's a record.' The cause of death was given as 'insult to the brain'.

CODA

I PRESUME THAT the late-developing novelist PENELOPE FITZGER-
ALD (née Knox, 1916-2000) must have come fairly often to the city in
the 1970s and early 80s, for her excellent novel *Innocence* (1986) is carefully and accurately set in 1950s Florence. But Hermione Lee's biography
of Mrs Fitzgerald, otherwise so informative, is not helpful on this point.

The Scottish novelist and poet MURIEL SPARK (née Camberg, 1918-2006)
moved from New York in the later 1960s to Rome, where in 1968 she met
the artist and sculptor Penelope Jardine. A few years later the two friends
settled into Miss Jardine's house at Oliveto in southern Tuscany. Muriel
Spark was the third of three internationally known Catholic novelists
who were close friends of Harold Acton—the other two being Evelyn
Waugh and Graham Greene. Between 1979 and 1992 she came about ten
times to Villa La Pietra, and she also dined together with Harold at John
Pope-Hennessy's flat in via de' Bardi. Like many people she disliked the
saltless Florentine bread, and advised the journalist Hunter Davies to put
salt on his. After the publication of her 'Lord Lucan' novel *Aiding and
Abetting* (2000), she gave a sparkling reading from it at the British Institute
of Florence.

The future critic and novelist FRANCIS KING (1923-2011) first came to Florence
on holiday, after taking his degree in English at Balliol College, Oxford,
in 1949. While in Florence he received a letter from the British Council,
offering to second him to the British Institute of Florence. He accepted
with enthusiasm, and the Council paid his salary: 'Had my colleagues [at
the British Institute in Palazzo Antinori] been less agreeable, this could
have been a source of unpleasantness between us, since, far younger and

Muriel Spark

Francis King

far less experienced than they, I was none the less paid far more.' Francis stayed at the Pensione Jennings-Riccioli on the lungarno delle Grazie, in the same building as the Pensione Simi where E.M. Forster had his room with a view. 'I can remember how, on my first evening in Florence, I wandered through the streets listening, in delighted incredulity, to the sound of people laughing all around me—at the tables of outdoor cafés, under the arches of the Ponte Vecchio, even at tram stops. It was extraordinarily rare to hear public laughter in England, except in derision.' After a few weeks in the pensione, Francis found himself 'a tiny flat, at the top of a gaunt building in the then working-class Via Parioncino, which was the property of a charming woman, previously lady-in-waiting to the Duchess of Aosta, Daisy Martinucci. Since Signorina Martinucci's morals were beyond reproach, it was a mystery why her flat, full of elaborate gilt-framed mirrors, pink bows, pink lampshades and pale blue and pink flounces, should so much resemble that of a tart.' After this Francis moved into a large villa near the Poggio Imperiale, which he shared with the talented and good-looking Michael Swan, whose sad end—he was crippled by a bungled attempt at suicide, before finally succeeding—is described in Francis's autobiography, *Yesterday Came Suddenly* (1993).

His eighteen months in the city provided Francis King with material for his Florentine novel *The Ant Colony* (1991). An ant colony in a glass case was the present that he had given to poor Michael Swan in order to cheer him up: 'He was so much fascinated by it, staring down at the teeming life of the ants, that he paid no attention to me, until I got up to go. Then… he emitted a strange, desolate wail.'

Later in life Francis wrote his useful and well informed *Florence: a Literary Companion* (1991), which was savagely and unfairly reviewed by Antony Lambton. The cigar-smoking, dark-glasses-wearing owner of Villa Cetinale later claimed that he had no idea Francis King was an eminent writer, but thought he must be a young whippersnapper who needed to be taught a lesson.

William Trevor

In June 1987 the Irish novelist and short-story writer WILLIAM TREVOR (real name William Trevor Cox, 1928-2016) came to the British Institute and read two suitably contrasting stories, 'Teresa's Wedding' and 'Two More Gallants'. This was a memorable occasion. I believe that Trevor either owned or rented property in Tuscany, for several of his Chekhovian short stories have Tuscan settings, such as the sinister 'Cocktails at Doney's', set in Florence. The staff of the British Institute made a *bella figura* when he visited the Library because they were able to put on display no fewer than thirty-one of his well-thumbed books, and he looked very pleased.

Towards the end of Harold Acton's life, in the early 1990s, more or less the only visitors he would receive at La Pietra were JOHN POPE-HENNESSY (1913-1994) and JOAN HASLIP (1912-1994). The three of them would sit around giggling and gossiping for hours. Pope-Hennessy was an immensely accomplished art historian and museum director whose magisterial pronouncements led to his being called 'the Pope'; he lived in Palazzo Canigiani in via de' Bardi as a tenant of the Capponi family; he wrote a three-volume history of Italian sculpture and an exemplary monograph on Donatello. In 1936 Berenson had called him 'the budding or rather dawning new grand lama of British art criticism.' Joan Haslip produced

Joan Haslip   *John Pope-Hennessy*

a couple of novels and a string of frothy romantic biographies; she lived as a child at Villa Le Rose and was educated in Florence; she had a flat in Bellosguardo, as a tenant of the Ricasoli family; to her victims she was known as 'Sharplip'. All three of them—Sir Harold, Sir John, Miss Haslip—died in the same year, 1994, which for that reason seems to me to mark the end of an era.

ACKNOWLEDGEMENTS

For help or inspiration or both, I thank Bruno d'Avanzo, Marta Baiardi, Fanny and Robin Blake, Edward Chaney, Laura Crackanthorpe, Nicholas Dakin-Elliot, Anthony Eyre, Jonathan Galassi, Katerine Gaja, Thomas Galdy, Simon Hewett, Suor Julia Holloway, Sally Hood, Penelope Jardine, Peter Kennealy, Alta Macadam, Philip Mansel, David Platzer, Alyson Price, Felix Roberts, Jean Schofield, William Scott Moncrieff and Flavio Tuliozi. For the earlier period I found much useful material in Clara Louise Dentler's pioneering study *Famous Foreigners in Florence, 1400-1900*, published in 1964 by Bemporad Marzocco.

ILLUSTRATIONS

View of Florence. Detail. Artist: Thomas Cole (Cleveland Museum of Art/Wikimedia).

John Hawkwood by Paolo Uccello. Florence Cathedral (Wikimedia).

Tribuna of the Uffizi Johan Zoffany. Royal Collections Trust (Wikimedia).

British gentlemen at Sir Horace Mann's house in Florence by Thomas Patch, ca 1765. Whereabouts unknown (Wikimedia).

Horace Walpole Portrait by Jonathan Richardson the Elder (Casa-Museu Medeiros e Almeida/Wikimedia).

Tobias Smollett Portrait in *The adventures of Sir Launcelot Greaves*; and *The history and adventures of an atom.* Artist unknown. (Wikimedia).

Thomas Patch Self-portrait, from a bound volume of 52 portrait caricatures, ca 1770 (Biblioteca Riccardiana-Moreniana, Florence).

The Gore Family with George, 3rd Earl Cowper Johan Zoffany (Google Art Project/Yale Center for British Art).

Edward Gibbon Henry Walton, 1774 (NPG, London/Wikimedia).

Edward Gibbon crossing the Alps (Guise Family Archive, Elmore Court).

Hester Lynch Thrale (Mrs Piozzi) (Thomas Pennant's *A Tour in Wales*, 1781).

William Beckford Engraving after portrait by Joshua Reynolds.

Boboli Gardens. Florence by Pierre Gauthiez (The Medici Society, 1927).

View of Florence Engraved by Goodall after painting by JMW Turner. From *Italy, a Poem* (1830) by Samuel Rogers.

Walter Savage Landor engraving after a photograph by Herbert Watkins (*Illustrated London News*, 15 October 1864).

Maguerite, Countess of Blessington Thomas Lawrence, 1822 (Wallace Collection/Wikimedia).

Interior of Palazzo Giugni-Fraschetti (Sailko/Wikimedia).

William Hazlitt Engraving of an 1825 portrait by William Bewick (Wikimedia).

Leigh Hunt portrayed in *The Maclise Portrait-Gallery of "Illustrious Literary Characters"* (1883).

James Fennimore Cooper Artist unknown. Wikimedia.

Percy Bysshe Shelley Shown writing *Prometheus Unbound*: posthumous portrait by Joseph Severn. Keats-Shelley Memorial House, Rome/Wikimedia.

Mary Wollstonecraft Shelley Richard Rothwell, 1840 (Drgn 1900/Wikimedia).

Edward Trelawny W.E. West. (British Museum/Wikimedia).

Thomas Macaulay Wood engraving after a photogravure by Antoine Claudet. (Wikimedia).

Beaujolais Campbell, Viscountess Tullamore Engraving. (Martin2001/Etsy).

Interior of Palazzo Giugni-Fraschetti (Sailko/Wikimedia.)

William Hazlitt Engraving of an 1825 portrait of William Hazlitt by William Bewick (Wikimedia).

Leigh Hunt Portrayed in *The Maclise Portrait-Gallery of "Illustrious Literary Characters"* (1883).

James Fennimore Cooper Artist unknown. (Wikimedia.)

Percy Bysshe Shelley Shown writing *Prometheus Unbound*: posthumous portrait by Joseph Severn. (Keats-Shelley Memorial House, Rome/Wikimedia.)

Mary Wollstonecraft Shelley Portrait by Richard Rothwell, 1840, in the National Portrait Gallery, London (Drgn 1900/Wikimedia).

Edward Trelawny Portrait by W.E. West (British Museum/Wikimedia).

Thomas Macaulay Wood engraving after a photogravure by Antoine Claudet (Wikimedia).

Beaujolais Campbell, Viscountess Tullamore (Martin2001/Etsy).

Nathaniel Hawthorne By Charles Osgood (Peabody Essex Museum, Salem).

Charles Lever Illustration from *The Cyclopedia of Wit and Humour*, New York 1875.

The Drawing Room at Casa Guidi Painting by Giorgio Mignaty commissioned by Robert Browning shortly after Elizabeth's death (vcrfl-blog.tumblr.com/ post/20647912490/giorgio-mignaty-casa-guidi).

The Brownings Portraits by Thomas B. Read (Christie's).

Henry Wadsworth Longfellow Daguerreotype, Southworth & Hawes (Metropolitan Museum of Art, New York/Wikimedia).

Alfred, Lord Tennyson By John Everett Millais (Private Collection/GetArchive).

Margaret Fuller (Wikimedia).

William Makepeace Thackery Print, after a drawing by Samuel Laurence (Wikimedia).

Charles Dickens 1843, portrait by Margaret Gillies (Philip Mould & Co Ltd).

Effects of the Plague Tableau by Gaetano Giulio Zumbo, ca 1691 (Natural History Museum, La Specola).

Anthony Trollope Photo by Napoleon Sarony (New York Public Library/Wikimedia).

Isabella Blagden Photographer unknown (Wikimedia).

John Ruskin From *The Works of John Ruskin* 1900.

Villa Palmieri Engraved by Giuseppe Zocchi 1744 (Wikimedia).

Hermann Melville Painted by Joseph Oriel Eaton (Houghton Library, Harvard University/Wikimedia).

George Eliot Photogravure from a painting by M. d'Albert-Durade (Wikimedia).

Fra Gerolamo Savonarola preaching Woodcut from his tract, *Compendio di Rivelazione* Florence 1495

Florence Nightingale Photo by Henry Hering (NPG, London/Wikimedia).

Monument to Florence Nightingale Santa Croce church, Florence. Sculptor: Francis William Sargant, 1913. (Wikimedia/Manuela Rossi).

Matthew Arnold By Elliott & Fry, published by Bickers & Son (Wikimedia).

Alfred Austin From *The Autobiography of Alfred Austin, Poet Laureate, 1835-1910* London: Macmillan (Wikimedia).

Mark Twain Portrait by A. F. Bradley, New York, 1907 (Wikimedia).

Oscar Browning Cartoon by "Hay" published 24 November 1888 in *Vanity Fair* (Wikimedia).

Algernon Charles Swinburne Drawing by Dante Gabriel Rossetti, 1862 (Ebay).

Kate Field "Kate Field at Glen Haven – Skaneateles" (wordpress.com).

Villa Stibbert Stibbert Museum, Florence (elisarolle.com).

Ouida Photograph by George G. Rockwood (New York Public Library/Wikimedia).

Walter Pater Cartoon by John Hearn, reproduced in *The Life of Walter Pater* by Thomas Wright, 1907 (Wikimedia).

Thomas Hardy Bain News Service/Library of Congress (Wikimedia).

Janet Ross (Maria Millarte, aroundmeblog.com).

Henry James By William M. Vander Weyde (George Eastman House Collection).

Oscar Wilde By Napoleon Sarony (Library of Congress/Wikimedia).

Verrnon Lee By John Singer Sargent (Tate Britain London).

The castle of Acciaiuoli at Montegufoni (Alinari Archives, Florence).

Sir George Sitwell Photographer unknown(https://theesotericcuriosa.blogspot.com/2009/11/honorary-esoteric-sir-george-reresby.html).

Osbert Sitwell The Bookman Volume 57 December 1919 (Wikimedia).

Edith Wharton By E. F. Cooper (Yale University/Wikimedia).

Ada Leverson By Elliot & Fry (Ryerson University Centre for Digital Humanities).

Charles Loeser (izi.travel/en/ce5e-biography-of-charles-loeser/en).

Herbert Horne Henry Harris Brown, *Herbert P. Horne*, 1908 (Florence, Museo Horne).

Horne Museum (Museo Horne, Florence).

Robert Langton Douglas (Douglas Archives)

Bernard Berenson The Critic Vol XLVI, June 1905 (Wikimedia).

Berenson outside Villa I Tatti Photographer unknown (Wikimedia).

Arnold Bennett By Pirie Macdonald, *When Winter Comes to Main Street* (New York, 1922; Wikimedia).

Norman Douglas By Carl Van Vechten (Library of Congress/Wikimedia).

Reginald Turner By Carl Van Vechten (Library of Congress/Wikimedia).

W. Somerset Maugham By Carl Van Vechten (Library of Congress/Wikimedia).

Edward Hutton (Source unknown).

Mabel Dodge Luhan By Carl Van Vechten (Library of Congress/Wikimedia).

EM Forster By George Platt Lynes, 1947 (Chiswick Auctions).

Virginia Woolf By George Charles Beresford (Wikimedia).

James Joyce By Alex Ehrenzweig (Wikimedia).

Harry Sinclair Lewis By Oscar Whiite (NPG Washington, Wikimedia).

DH Lawrence Passport photograph (Wikimedia).

Geoffrey Scott and Cecil Pinsent (Courtesy of Dr John Scott/elisarolle.com).

Edith Sitwell Published in *The Last Years of a Rebel* by Elisabeth Salter (Bodley Head, 1967).

Charles Kenneth Scott-Moncrieff (Scotclans.com).

Richard Aldington By Howard Coster. (NPG London/Wikimedia)

Aldous Huxley (Flickr/Antonio Marin Segovia)

Evelyn Waugh By Carl Van Vechten (Library of Congress/Wikimedia).

Kenneth Clark By Gerty Simon (*The Guardian*).

Harold Acton (Harold Acton: memorie di un esteta cattolico | Radio Spada).

Villa La Pietra (Harold Acton: memorie di un esteta cattolico | Radio Spada).

Graham Greene (*New Statesman*).

Nancy Mitford (*Vanity Fair*).

Dylan Thomas (Wikimedia).

Muriel Spark (British Council).

Francis King Publicity photo (Wikimedia).

William Trevor (Jonkers Rare Books).

Joan Haslip By Francis Goodman (© NPG London).

John Pope-Hennessy (Arnold Newman Papers and Photography Collection, Harry Ransom Center, The University of Texas at Austin).

INDEX